American English

Personal Best

Workbook

A2
Elementary

Series Editor
Jim Scrivener

Author
Genevieve White

You and me

GRAMMAR: The verb *be*

1 Choose the correct options to complete the sentences.

1 I *am / is / are* nineteen years old.
2 She *am / is / are* a teacher.
3 *Am / is / Are* you from this country?
4 They *am not / isn't / aren't* at home.
5 We *am / is / are* all in the same class.
6 *Am / Is / Are* she English?
7 I *'m not / isn't / aren't* hungry.
8 It *am / is / are* nice to meet you.

2 Complete the sentences with the correct form of the verb *be*.

1 "Where's Malu?" "I don't know. She _____ here."
2 "Are you twenty?" "No, I _____ twenty-two."
3 My parents _____ in New York this week.
4 "Is Pablo your brother?" "No. He _____ my friend."
5 "Where are the children?" "They _____ at home. They're at school."
6 "_____ we all here?" "No, James is in the classroom."
7 You _____ a teacher. You're a student.
8 "_____ she Russian?" "No, she's Polish."

VOCABULARY: Numbers 1–1000, countries, and nationalities

3 Write the words or numbers.

1 95 _____
2 twenty-one _____
3 47 _____
4 two thousand _____
5 12 _____
6 six hundred and thirty _____
7 802 _____
8 eighty-five _____
9 13 _____
10 fifteen _____

4 Match flags a–f with nationalities 1–6.

a   b   c

d   e   f

1 Swedish _____
2 Chinese _____
3 Australian _____
4 Argentinian _____
5 Vietnamese _____
6 Turkish _____

5 Complete the sentences with countries or nationalities.

1 My mom's from Japan. She's _____.
2 Our teacher is from _____. She's Canadian.
3 I'm from Ireland. I'm _____.
4 His best friend is from _____. She's Italian.
5 Marta is from Portugal. She's _____.
6 My dad's from the U.S. He's _____.
7 They are _____. They're from Brazil.
8 We are from Spain. We're _____.
9 Michel's _____. He's from France.
10 Wahid is from Egypt. He's _____.

PRONUNCIATION: Contractions of *be*

6 ▶1.1 Underline the contractions. Say the sentences. Listen, check, and repeat.

1 "Are you eighteen years old?" "No, I'm twenty."
2 "Where is Miguel?" "He's in a meeting."
3 This is the café. We're eating breakfast here.
4 Anna is my sister. She's an English teacher.
5 They're my friends. We are in the same class.
6 I know you. You're Sasha's brother.
7 "Is your car German?" "No, it's Italian."

READING: Approaching a text

My trip with the orchestra

Hi! I'm Paula, and I'm from Portugal. I ¹_____ a student, but I'm also in a guitar orchestra for young people. Right now, I'm on a trip with the orchestra. We're ready to play concerts in London, Paris, and Rome! Here's my blog about my month of music.

WEEK 1

These are some of my friends from the orchestra. They ²_____ a lot of fun! Marina ³_____ nineteen, and Miguel is eighteen. They're my best friends. We usually go to the park together – we all like nature. We're in London right now, and there are lots of beautiful parks here.

WEEK 2

Our guitar teacher's name is Carlos, and he's very friendly. He is a great teacher – and he also cooks dinner for us every night. We all like his food very much.

WEEK 3

We ⁴_____ in Paris now, at a hotel downtown. There are a lot of English students in this hotel, so I practice my English every day. The orchestra plays music every morning until noon, and then we walk around the city. It's a really interesting place, and we see and do lots of things.

WEEK 4

We're in Rome now. It ⁵_____ an exciting city! Our concerts ⁶_____ in the evening, and we go shopping every day. My month of music is nearly finished. I'm happy because I want to see my family, but I'm sad because this trip is great.

1 Look at the title, headings, and pictures. Choose the best description for the text.

  a Someone who goes to music school every day.

  b Someone who travels with her orchestra for four weeks.

  c Someone who visits Rome on vacation.

2 Complete the text with the correct forms of the verb *be*.

3 Are the sentences true (T), false (F), or doesn't say (DS)?

  1 Paula is Portuguese. _____

  2 Her friend Marina is Spanish. _____

  3 There are nice parks in London. _____

  4 Carlos is a bad cook. _____

  5 There are no French students in the hotel in Paris. _____

  6 Miguel doesn't like Paris. _____

  7 Paula likes Rome. _____

  8 Marina and Miguel like shopping in Rome. _____

GRAMMAR: Possessive adjectives and 's for possession

1 Choose the correct options to complete the sentences.

1 My classmates and I all like _____ English teacher.
   a our   **b** his   **c** their

2 "What is your _____ name?" "Her name's Giulia."
   a sisters   **b** sisters'   **c** sister's

3 "Is this _____ key?" "Yes – it's mine."
   a my   **b** your   **c** her

4 Do you like _____ shoes? They're new!
   a Jame's   **b** James   **c** James'

5 "Where does Enrico live?" "_____ house is over there."
   a Its   **b** His   **c** Your

6 "Is Emma at home?" "No. Her _____ car's not here."
   a parents   **b** parent's   **c** parents'

7 I have a white cat. _____ name is Snowy.
   a My   **b** Their   **c** Its

8 This store doesn't have _____ bags.
   a womens   **b** women's   **c** womens'

2 Complete the text with possessive adjectives.

Juan

I'm Juan, and this is a photo of ¹_____ class. You can see my best friend – ²_____ name's Marta – and ³_____ teacher. ⁴_____ name is Pedro, and he has two children. ⁵_____ names are Luisa and Carlos.

This is a photo of my house. Mom and I live here. It's a small house, but ⁶_____ garden is pretty big – we both like gardening! We have a cat, too – ⁷_____ name is Sooty because it is black and white. What about you? What are ⁸_____ friends and house like?

VOCABULARY: Personal objects

3 Match definitions 1–6 with objects a–f.

1 You can see your face in this.   _____
2 You open a door with this.   _____
3 You can talk to your friends with it.   _____
4 You wear these on your hands when it's cold.   _____
5 You need this when it rains.   _____
6 You put your money in it.   _____

   a umbrella
   b change purse
   c phone
   d gloves
   e key
   f mirror

4 Complete the words.

1 This is a p __ __ __ __ of me with my mom and my sister. We are on vacation!

2 You can buy a s __ __ __ __ for your postcard at the post office.

3 What time is it? I don't have a w __ __ __ __.

4 When I walk at night, I take a f __ __ __ __ __ __ __ __ __ to help me see.

5 My name and address are on my i __ __ __ __ __ __ __ c __ __ __.

6 I eat a lot of c __ __ __ __. My mom says it's bad for my teeth.

7 I can't read this without my g __ __ __ __ __ __.

8 We can't have c __ __ __ __ __ g __ __ during class.

PRONUNCIATION: Sentence stress

5 ▶ 1.2 Listen and repeat the sentences. <u>Underline</u> the stressed words in each sentence. Listen again, check, and repeat.

1 What's in his wallet?
2 Here are your books.
3 My tablet is on the chair.
4 What's her name?
5 Their house is new.
6 Where are my tissues?

SPEAKING: Asking for and giving personal information

1 ▶1.3 Listen to the conversation. Which sentence is correct?

A Miguel is at home.
B Miguel is on the phone.
C Miguel is at the gym.

2 ▶1.3 Listen again. Complete the sentences.

1 What's your f_____ name?
2 And what's your _____?
3 Do you have an _____ address, Miguel?
4 And what's your _____ number, please?
5 What's your a_____?
6 OK. What's your z_____?

3 ▶1.3 Listen again and complete the form below.

4 ▶1.3 Does the receptionist ask for clarification for Miguel's information? Listen again and write A, B, or C for 1–6. There may be more than one answer.

A Yes, she asks, "How do you spell that (please)?"
B Yes, she asks Miguel to repeat information.
C No, she doesn't ask for clarification.

1 first name ____
2 last name ____
3 e-mail address ____
4 cell phone number ____
5 address ____
6 zip code ____

5 ▶1.4 Look at the information on the form below. Listen and check if it is correct. Ask for clarification and make sure you use polite intonation.

SUPERFIT GYM Date:

CLIENT INFORMATION

First name:

Last name:

CONTACT DETAILS

E-mail:
@starmail.com

Phone number:
917

Address:
8   Street

Zip code:

SUPERFIT GYM Date:

CLIENT INFORMATION

First name:
MARIA

Last name:
PALMA

CONTACT DETAILS

E-mail:
palma90@newmail.com

Phone number:
215-555-0079

Address:
527 Queen Road

Zip code:
19147

HOME   BLOG   PODCASTS   ABOUT   CONTACT

Learning Curve

Tom and Sam talk about an interesting street.

LISTENING

1 ▶ 1.5 Listen to the podcast about an interesting street. Read the sentences. Are they true (T) or false (F)?

1 Roosevelt Avenue is in the U.S. _____

2 It's interesting because it's a very international street. _____

3 Jacob's store sells stamps. _____

4 His mother is from Ireland. _____

5 Mr. Deng is Vietnamese. _____

6 He cooks and serves food. _____

7 Maria is Portuguese. _____

8 Anna is from India. _____

2 ▶ 1.5 Listen again. Complete the sentences with the numbers in the box. There are four numbers you don't need.

2	3	4	53	63
73	118	122	180	

1 Jacob's store sells _____ different kinds of candy.

2 People from _____ different countries live in the neighborhood.

3 Mr. Deng has _____ restaurants.

4 Maria has _____ children.

5 Anna has _____ sisters.

READING

1 Read the blog on page 7 about an international home. Write the people's nationalities.

1 Suki _____

2 Lucja _____

3 Ryan _____

4 Simona _____

5 Marco _____

2 Circle the countries in the blog and underline the personal objects.

3 Are the sentences true (T), false (F), or doesn't say (DS)?

1 Suki is from France. _____

2 Five people live in Suki's apartment. _____

3 Lucja speaks English well. _____

4 Suki is eighteen years old. _____

5 Ryan is a student. _____

6 Ryan works in a store in Paris. _____

7 Simona doesn't like the weather in Brazil. _____

8 Simona's family lives in Brazil. _____

9 Marco has a job in Paris. _____

10 Marco is Suki's boyfriend. _____

HOME **BLOG** PODCASTS ABOUT CONTACT

Guest blogger Penny writes about people living in another country.

AN INTERNATIONAL HOME

All around the world, young people live and study away from their own homes. But what's it like living with people from other countries? I asked Suki, a photography student. Suki's from Vietnam, but she lives in France now. Here's what she says about life in her international home.

I live in an apartment in Paris with four other people. We're all from different countries, but we can all speak English really well. Our apartment is very friendly, and, of course, it has a great international atmosphere!

Lucja is from Poland, and she's eighteen years old. She is a student, like me. She wants to be a dentist, but she really loves candy! Lucja's a very happy person – I like her a lot. Here's a photo of her looking happy.

Ryan is twenty-five years old, and he is from Ireland. He works in a café near our apartment. He likes shopping, and he loves shopping for clothes. Here's a photo of him wearing his favorite sunglasses. He thinks they are very cool!

Simona is from Brazil. She's twenty-one years old, and she's a nurse. She doesn't like the weather here – she is always cold! I think she is unhappy because she can't see her family back home very often, and she misses her son. Here's Simona with her favorite umbrella – she takes it everywhere she goes!

Marco is from Italy. He's a student, too, but he wants to be a model. He's very handsome, isn't he? He's 23 years old, and he likes cars, soccer, and looking in the mirror!

Who do you live with? Tell us about them and where you live. Don't forget to send us some photographs, too!

Work and play

2A — LANGUAGE

GRAMMAR: Simple present: affirmative and negative

1 Choose the correct options to complete the sentences.

1 He _____ a taxi every evening.
   a drives   b drive
   c don't drive

2 My sister _____ English – she teaches math.
   a teach   b doesn't teach
   c teaches

3 I like my job, but it _____ very well.
   a doesn't pay   b pays
   c pay

4 On the weekend, I'm a tour guide. I _____ tourists around my city.
   a doesn't take   b takes
   c take

5 I speak French, but I _____ German.
   a don't speak   b speaks
   c speak

6 My mom _____ in a restaurant. She serves food.
   a work   b works
   c don't work

2 Complete the e-mail with the correct simple present form of the verbs in parentheses.

Hi Malin,

How are you? I am very busy right now.
I ¹_____ (work) a lot of hours every day.

We ²_____ (have) a new teacher at school – Mrs. Black. She ³_____ (teach) us English and French. She's very funny – everyone ⁴_____ (like) her. Mrs. Black loves movies, and we ⁵_____ (watch) a lot of interesting videos in her class. She ⁶_____ (live) near here, though – she drives from Boston every day!

Mom and dad say "hello"! They are busy, too. The restaurant is very popular, and they ⁷_____ (serve) food and drink all day, every day!

Write soon,

Tamara

VOCABULARY: Jobs and job verbs

3 Order the letters to make words for jobs.

1 My mom's a TRODCO. She works in a hospital.
   _____

2 I'm a student, but on Friday nights I'm a GISREN with my band.
   _____

3 Ask a CAIMNECH to look at your car.
   _____

4 You must be good at math to work as an TONCANACUT.
   _____

5 I love traveling, so I want to be a THIGLF NETTANDTA.
   _____

6 I need to go to the STINTED. My teeth hurt.
   _____

7 My sister works as a TOESCIRENPIT in a hotel.
   _____

8 This light is broken. I have to call an CAINCLEETRI.
   _____

4 Complete the sentences with job verbs.

1 Julio is a waiter. He _____ food in a restaurant.
2 My hairdresser _____ my hair every month.
3 Her aunt is a salesclerk. She _____ computers in a big store.
4 He always _____ a suit to work because he's a lawyer.
5 Sonia is a tour guide. She _____ tourists with their questions.
6 His brother is a famous chef. He _____ food in the best hotel in Rome.

PRONUNCIATION: -s and -es endings

5 ▶ 2.1 Listen and circle the sound that you hear at the end of the underlined verb. Listen again, check, and repeat.

	/s/	/z/	/ɪz/
1 Suki <u>works</u> in a restaurant.	/s/	/z/	/ɪz/
2 Anna <u>watches</u> TV every day.	/s/	/z/	/ɪz/
3 Sally <u>helps</u> her brother with his homework.	/s/	/z/	/ɪz/
4 Jean Paul <u>drives</u> an Italian car.	/s/	/z/	/ɪz/
5 Ester really <u>likes</u> chocolate.	/s/	/z/	/ɪz/
6 Roberto <u>lives</u> in Argentina.	/s/	/z/	/ɪz/
7 Max <u>teaches</u> science.	/s/	/z/	/ɪz/
8 Turgay <u>sells</u> shoes.	/s/	/z/	/ɪz/

LISTENING: Listening for names, places, days, and times

1 ▶ 2.2 Listen to the conversation between two friends. Which names and places do you hear?

	a		b		c	
1	a	Janine	b	Jenny	c	Joan
2	a	Donna	b	Donald	c	Danny
3	a	Mateo's	b	Maria's	c	Marco's
4	a	Boston	b	Houston	c	Stockton
5	a	Vicky	b	Vinny	c	Ricky

2 ▶ 2.2 Complete the sentences with *in*, *on*, or *at*. Then listen again and check.

1 Vanessa plays tennis _____ seven o'clock.
2 She eats pizza _____ the Italian restaurant.
3 _____ Thursday night, she studies.
4 She is always _____ Boston on Friday evenings.
5 Paul watches TV _____ Saturday evening.
6 Paul's favorite TV show starts _____ eight o'clock.

3 Match the words to make activities.

1	play	_____	a	friends
2	read	_____	b	to music
3	meet	_____	c	the guitar
4	spend time	_____	d	English
5	go out	_____	e	a movie
6	see	_____	f	with my family
7	study	_____	g	for dinner
8	listen	_____	h	the newspaper

4 Complete the sentences with six of the activities from exercise 3. Use the correct form of the verbs. Use affirmative and negative forms.

1 She's the singer in the band, and she also _____.
2 I _____ at home. I don't have a favorite group.
3 They _____ every day. They know a lot about the world.
4 She _____ at the new language school downtown.
5 We _____ every week. We really like Italian restaurants.
6 Now that I am in college, I _____ except on vacation.

5 ▶ 2.3 Read the sentences. Underline the words that only have the sound /ə/. Then listen and check.

1 Do you like music?
2 My sister's a teacher.
3 I want to play tennis!
4 What do you do in your free time?
5 He goes to school on Saturday morning.
6 Where is the movie theater?

GRAMMAR: Simple present: questions

1 Complete the sentences with the words in the box.

> what do who does (x 2) how
> when where don't (x 2)

1 _____ you play soccer?
2 "Does she work here?" "Yes, she _____."
3 _____ do you go after work?
4 "Do they like dogs?" "No, they _____."
5 _____ does he live with?
6 _____ does class start?
7 _____ your father speak Italian?
8 "Do you know Lisa?" "No, we _____."
9 _____ do they do on the weekend?
10 _____ do you say this word?

2 Order the words to make questions.

1 does / study / where / he / Turkish
_____?

2 Vietnam / you / come from / do
_____?

3 she / a cat / does / have
_____?

4 with / they / who / do / go out
_____?

5 at / do / start work / eight / we
_____?

6 you / do / why / to school / drive
_____?

7 does / fix / where / she / cars
_____?

8 suit / wear / he / a / does
_____?

PRONUNCIATION: Auxiliary *do/does* in questions

3 Look at the pictures. Use the prompts to write questions about Carla.

1 where/live?
_____

2 how/work?
_____

3 when/home?
_____

4 do/study/evening?
_____

5 what/weekends?
_____

6 who/movies?
_____

4 ▶ 2.4 Say the questions. How do we say *do* and *does*? Listen, check, and repeat.

1 Do you like pizza?
2 Does he live with his parents?
3 What do you do on the weekend?
4 Do they speak Spanish?
5 Where does he work?
6 When do you watch TV?
7 Does your sister teach yoga?
8 Who do you spend time with in the evening?

WRITING: Opening and closing an informal e-mail

Hey Lucy,

How are things with you? Do you like your new home in New York?

Here in Madrid, everything is fine. I have a new roommate. She is really nice and friendly, but I often think of you and wish you were here! Her name is Keira, and she's from New Zealand. She's a good cook, but she doesn't make great chocolate cake like you!

I have a new part-time job. I'm a tour guide – I take people around Madrid and show them the sights. I work every afternoon, from 2 p.m. till 6 or 7 p.m. I really like my job, but I don't have a lot of free time right now! You can see me working in this photo.

In the evenings, I am pretty tired, but I sometimes play tennis with Keira. On weekends, I usually go to the movies or go shopping.

Take care,

María

1 Read María's e-mail then look at the phrases below. Are they opening (O) or closing (C) phrases?

1 Hi _____
2 Write soon _____
3 See you soon _____
4 Hello _____
5 Hi Marta _____
6 Love, Freddie XXX _____

2 Find and <u>underline</u> the connectors in the e-mail.

3 Choose the correct connectors.

1 I really like coffee, *and / but* I don't like tea at all.
2 Is that your mother, *and / or* is it your sister?
3 I go to school, *and / so* I also have extra English classes.
4 I'm from Spain, *but / and* I now live in Mexico.
5 I have two sisters: Vanessa *and / or* Sally.
6 Are you a teacher *or / but* a student?

4 Complete the e-mail with *and*, *but*, or *or*.

Hi Samantha,

I'm on vacation in Granada in Spain. Our vacation is really fun ¹_____ exciting, ²_____ I wish you were here. I think it's the perfect place for you. You can choose to go to the beach ³_____ the mountains. The food ⁴_____ drinks are delicious, ⁵_____ people have lunch too late! They don't eat until 3 o'clock!

I will call you soon ⁶_____ write another e-mail.

Bye,

Clare

5 Write an e-mail to a friend in another country. Use *and*, *but*, and *or* to connect your ideas. Include:

• an informal opening phrase
• information about your home, friends, and free time
• an informal closing phrase.

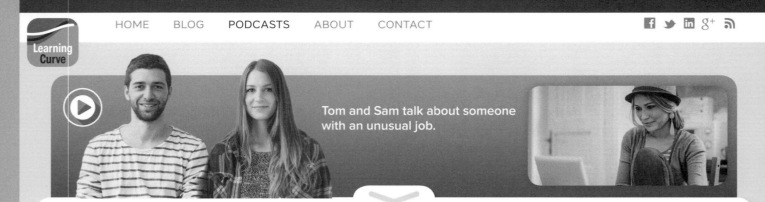

Tom and Sam talk about someone with an unusual job.

LISTENING

1 ▶ 2.5 Listen to the podcast about someone with an interesting job. Choose the correct answers.

1 Which sentence about Arabella is true?
a She doesn't like going to the movies.
b Her hobby is also her job.
c She reads a lot of newspapers.

2 What is Arabella's job?
a She sells tickets at a movie theater.
b She's the manager of a magazine.
c She writes about movies.

3 What does Arabella say about Luke?
a He really likes movies.
b He is her friend.
c He doesn't talk a lot.

2 ▶ 2.5 Listen again. Complete the sentences with one or two words.

1 Arabella really loves her _____.

2 She writes about movies for _____ and magazines.

3 She goes to the movies _____ times a week.

4 She really likes horror _____.

5 After she sees a movie, she likes to _____ it.

6 She also writes about _____.

3 ▶ 2.5 Order the words to make questions. Listen again and check your answers.

1 go / do / you / every night / to the movies ?
_____

2 what kind / like / you / do / of movies ?
_____

3 you / take / with you / a friend / do ?
_____

4 have / you / do / another job ?
_____

READING

1 Read the blog on page 13 about work and free time. Answer the questions.

1 What is Tom Fletcher's job?

2 Does Tom think we have a good work-life balance?

3 What does Tom think we need to spend more time doing?

2 Does Tom say the things below? Choose Yes or No.

1	Many people start work at seven o'clock.	Yes	No
2	People work more hours in winter.	Yes	No
3	Tom has his lunch at home.	Yes	No
4	Many people always feel tired.	Yes	No
5	Playing the guitar can make you feel good.	Yes	No
6	Meeting friends is a good idea.	Yes	No
7	We have to all walk for fifteen minutes every day.	Yes	No
8	More free time is also good for your family.	Yes	No

3 Circle the free-time activities in the blog.

HOME **BLOG** PODCASTS ABOUT CONTACT

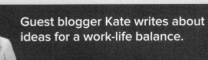

Guest blogger Kate writes about ideas for a work-life balance.

Work or life?

Today, lots of people work or study for more than 50 hours a week. We don't have much free time during the week. But it's important to have a "work-life balance" and to have some time away from work and studying. What can we do to make sure we don't work too much? Here are some ideas from life coach, Tom Fletcher.

People work really hard these days. Think about it – most of us read our work e-mails before breakfast! Then we work until seven o'clock. In the winter, we probably don't see the sun! Sixty percent of us take work home, too – and check our work e-mails late at night.

This is what a lot of people tell me about their day: "I get up at six o'clock, eat lunch at my desk, and go home at ten o'clock at night. I don't have time to go to a restaurant or to meet friends. I don't spend time with my family either – I'm always too busy. I want to relax, but there's not enough time during the day. I'm always tired, and I don't really enjoy my life right now."

This isn't good for our minds or bodies. You need to make time for life, because it's important to do things that you enjoy. Listen to music, play the guitar, read a book or go to the movies – these are things that make you feel good. And when you feel good, you can also work better.

Free-time activities don't need a lot of time – it's easy to make small changes to your day. Do you eat your lunch at your desk? Why not go out to a café – it's much more fun! Try to meet friends every day. Go for a fifteen-minute walk together. It makes you feel great and gives you more energy!

People in my life

3A LANGUAGE

GRAMMAR: Frequency adverbs and expressions

1 Order the words to make sentences.

1 always / is / your sister / late for school

_____.

2 together / eats dinner / our family / once a week

_____.

3 grandparents / sees / his / he / twice a month

_____.

4 because / play tennis / I / never / I don't like it

_____.

5 breakfast / they / eat / sometimes / a big

_____.

6 in the kitchen / a day / helps my mother / my brother / three times

_____.

2 Complete the conversation with adverbs and frequency expressions.

Anas	What do you ¹u_____ during the summer vacation?
Sara	I travel to the U.S. ²o_____ a year.
Anas	You're so lucky!
Sara	Well, my family lives there, and I don't ³o_____ see them. But I visit my cousins ⁴t_____ a month because they live near me. What about you?
Anas	I stay home ⁵e_____ year.
Sara	Really? Isn't that boring?
Anas	Not at all! I work in a café three ⁶t_____ a week, and I see my friends every day.

VOCABULARY: Family

3 Match the two parts of the sentences.

1 My aunt _____
2 My mother-in-law _____
3 My nephew _____
4 My grandparents _____
5 My niece _____
6 My sister-in-law _____

  a is my husband's sister.
  b is my brother's son.
  c is my mother's sister.
  d is my wife's mother.
  e are my parents' mother and father.
  f is my sister's daughter.

4 Complete the family words.

This is a photo of my family. This is me. I have one ¹s_____. Her name's Sal, and this is her ²h_____, Ali. He's also my ³b_____-i_____-l_____, of course! They have two ⁴c_____ – both boys, named Casper and John – who are my ⁵n_____. My ⁶f_____ took the photo. His brother, Fred, is my favorite ⁷u_____!

PRONUNCIATION: Sentence stress

5 ▶ 3.1 Read the sentences. Stress the adverbs and frequency expressions. Listen, check, and repeat.

1 He sometimes visits his cousin.
2 We're never late.
3 I study English every day.
4 I see my nephew once a week.
5 We often eat Chinese food.
6 I usually go to the park with my niece.

READING: Scanning a text

VACATIONS WITH A DIFFERENCE!

IT'S VACATION TIME! READ ABOUT OUR ACTIVE VACATIONS
WHICH ONE DO YOU LIKE BEST?

A PONY HIKING

Our pony hiking vacations are very popular. On these vacations, you stay in a quiet hotel in a beautiful place. Then you get up early and go pony hiking until 3 p.m. with one of our friendly guides. You also learn all about pony care.

C TAKE A BREAK – WITH A YOGA VACATION

Are you busy at work? Are you always tired? Relax and spend time with other people who love yoga. You stay in a beautiful small house near the sea. In the morning, you practice yoga, and go swimming in the sea. In the afternoon and evening, you eat our healthy food (it's also delicious!).

B SINGING IN SUMMER!

Do you love music? Then this vacation is for you. On this special vacation, you sing in a group every morning for two hours. Then, in the afternoon, you give group concerts in the town center. In the evening, you relax and sometimes go dancing, too. It's a lot of fun!

D ARTS AND CRAFTS

Our arts and crafts vacation is for people who love to make things. Every morning you learn a different craft, and in the afternoon, you go on trips to visit different artists. In the evening, you show the other students your work. It's a fun vacation, and it's interesting, too!

1 Scan the text. On which vacation do you:

1 eat delicious food? _____
2 dance in the evenings? _____
3 stay in a hotel? _____
4 learn different crafts? _____

2 Are the sentences true (T), false (F), or doesn't say (DS)?

1 On the pony hiking vacation, you go riding with a guide. _____
2 You can go swimming in the evening on the pony hiking vacation. _____
3 You meet people from different countries on the singing vacation. _____
4 On the singing vacation, you can relax in the evenings. _____
5 You buy and cook your own food on the yoga vacation. _____

6 On the yoga vacation, you stay near the sea. _____
7 On the arts and crafts vacation, other people can look at your work. _____
8 You make different things in the afternoon on the arts and crafts vacation. _____

3 Complete the sentences with *also* or *too*.

1 These vacations sound good! I like the yoga vacation and the singing vacation, _____.
2 I want to go on the pony hiking vacations and I _____ want to go on the yoga vacation.
3 I like ponies, and I _____ like quiet hotels.
4 On the arts and crafts vacation, you make art, and you look at other people's work, _____.
5 Singing is fun, and it's relaxing, _____.
6 Yoga is interesting, and it's _____ very good for you.

GRAMMAR: *love, like, hate, enjoy, don't mind* + noun/*-ing* form

1 Complete the text with the *-ing* form of the verbs in parentheses.

I love ¹_____ (live) with my family! We're all very happy. My dad enjoys ²_____ (drive) his taxi for work every day. My mom's very busy, so I don't mind ³_____ (make) breakfast for my little sister and ⁴_____ (take) her to the park sometimes. My brother, Pat, loves ⁵_____ (run) in the park, and he really likes ⁶_____ (swim) in the outside pool there – but he hates ⁷_____ (go) to school! On the weekend, we all enjoy ⁸_____ (be) together. Sometimes I like to be alone though. I love ⁹_____ (sit) with a book or ¹⁰_____ (plan) my future!

2 Complete the sentences with *love / don't like / doesn't like / hate / enjoy / don't mind* + *-ing* form of the verbs in the box.

study help meet work spend
play go relax watch eat

1 Do you _____ time with your family on the weekend? ☺

2 I _____ vegetables, but I like French fries more! ☺

3 My sister _____ math and never does her homework. ☹☹

4 Do you _____ in the evening after work? ☺

5 We _____ our friends for coffee in the new café in town. ☺☺

6 Jaime _____ to the dentist, so he doesn't go very often. ☹☹

7 His uncle makes cars. He _____ in a factory. ☹

8 They _____ their mom with the shopping and cooking. ☺

9 I _____ movies at home, but I go to the movie theater every week. ☹

10 Does your brother _____ online games? ☺☺

VOCABULARY: Activities (2)

3 Order the letters to make words for activities.

1 OG PSHOPNIG

_____

2 OG OT A LLAGYRE

_____

3 LYAP HET LINVIO

_____

4 OG GLIBWON

_____

5 OD GOYA

_____

6 HEAV A CINCIP

_____

7 APLY LOVELYBLLA

_____

8 ISITV STERILAVE

_____

4 Complete the sentences with the correct verbs.

1 What great weather! Do you want to _____ a barbecue?

2 When it rains on vacation, I like to _____ to museums.

3 I never _____ golf – I think it's a boring game.

4 My girlfriend loves to _____ swimming, but I hate the water!

5 I don't have time to cook, so I often _____ a takeout for dinner.

6 I want to _____ dancing tonight. There's a great DJ playing!

7 Do you want to _____ bike riding on the weekend?

8 His niece wants to learn to _____ karate next year.

PRONUNCIATION: *-ing* forms

5 ▶3.2 Say the sentences. How do we say the *-ing* forms? Listen, check, and repeat.

1 I don't mind playing tennis.

2 We love visiting our grandmother.

3 I don't like being late.

4 I love reading stories.

5 I like running.

6 I hate watching TV.

7 I don't mind going to school.

8 I enjoy playing sports.

SPEAKING: Accepting or declining an invitation

1 Look at the clocks and write the times.

1 It's _____ .
2 It's _____ .
3 It's _____ .
4 It's _____ .
5 _____ .
6 _____ .
7 _____ .
8 _____ .

2 ▶ 3.3 Listen to the conversation between two friends. Are the sentences true or false?

1	Pablo suggests going for a walk.	True	False
2	Sara accepts Pablo's invitation for tonight.	True	False
3	Sara has to visit her grandfather.	True	False
4	Pablo suggests tomorrow morning.	True	False
5	They agree to meet at one o'clock.	True	False

3 ▶ 3.3 Complete the lines from the conversation with the words in the box. Then listen again and check.

how	let's	can't	time
say	about	plans	want

1 Do you have _____ after work today?
2 Do you _____ to go to the movies with me?
3 Tonight? Oh, I'm sorry, I _____ .
4 What _____ tomorrow?
5 _____ about having lunch with me?
6 Great, _____ go together.
7 What _____ is good for you?
8 Let's _____ one o'clock.

4 Match 1–5 with a–e to make conversations.

1 Do you want to come to my birthday party on Saturday? _____
2 Would you like to come to the game with me? I've got two tickets. _____
3 How about going to the new burger restaurant together? _____
4 Do you want to have coffee together later? _____
5 Are you free for lunch today? _____

a I'd love to, but I don't eat meat. Sorry!
b Cool! I love soccer.
c Sure!
d Yes, I'd love to!
e Saturday? I'm sorry, I can't.

5 ▶ 3.4 Listen and check. Then say if the people accept (A) or decline (D) the invitations in each conversation.

1 _____
2 _____
3 _____
4 _____
5 _____

6 ▶ 3.4 Listen again and repeat the conversations in exercise 4. Copy the intonation to sound enthusiastic or sorry.

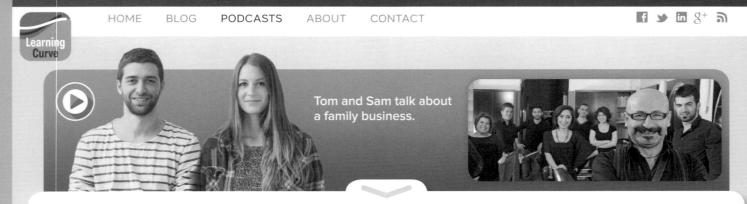

Tom and Sam talk about a family business.

LISTENING

1 ▶ 3.5 Listen to the podcast about a family business called "Swish." Number a–h in the order you hear them (1–8).

a brother ____

b sisters ____

c mother ____

d grandmother ____

e grandfather ____

f cousins ____

g sister-in-law ____

h aunts ____

2 ▶ 3.5 Listen again and choose the correct answers.

1 Why do people enjoy going to Swish?
  a The haircuts are very cheap.
  b The hairdressers are friendly.
  c There's a nice atmosphere.

2 How many family members work at the hairdresser?
  a ten
  b eleven
  c thirteen

3 How many aunts does Mila have?
  a two
  b three
  c four

4 What does Mila do at Swish?
  a She cuts hair.
  b She makes coffee.
  c She does lots of different things.

5 Does the family enjoy working together?
  a sometimes
  b usually
  c always

6 Why are there problems sometimes?
  a because of money
  b because of customers
  c because they are busy

READING

1 Read the blog on page 19 about spending time with your family. Write R (Roberto), M (Mariella), or B (both). Who:

1 doesn't like playing golf? ____

2 is busy at work? ____

3 likes going out with friends? ____

4 doesn't enjoy going dancing? ____

5 doesn't like shopping? ____

6 goes cycling three times a month? ____

2 Are the sentences true (T) or false (F)?

1 Roberto doesn't like music. ____

2 Mariella and Roberto hardly ever talk together. ____

3 Mariella plays golf with her friends. ____

4 Roberto likes playing golf with his daughter. ____

5 Roberto has a lot of free time. ____

6 Mariella and Roberto sometimes ride their bikes to the beach. ____

7 Mariella talks to her father about school. ____

8 Roberto enjoys going bike riding with Mariella. ____

3 Circle the adverbs and expressions of frequency in the blog.

HOME **BLOG** PODCASTS ABOUT CONTACT

Guest blogger Simon writes about how a father and a daughter spend time together.

Family time

In today's busy world, it's not always easy for families to spend time together. So why not try doing your mother's, father's, son's, or daughter's hobby with them? Read about how Mariella and her dad, Roberto, enjoy some free time together.

Mariella

My dad plays golf three times a week. He's always at the golf course. I don't know why! I don't think it's a great sport – you don't run, there's no music, and I don't like the clothes people wear!

I don't see my dad very often, and sometimes I don't know what to talk to him about. That's why I like coming here together, because there's always something to talk about – where the golf ball is going, for example! When we're at home, I'm usually on my phone talking to friends. But I never look at my phone when we play golf!

I play golf with Dad about once a week. I don't really like it very much, but I like being with him, and I know he enjoys it, too.

Roberto

I have a very busy job, and I hardly ever have free time. But Mariella doesn't talk to me often. She has a lot of friends, and she enjoys going out with them. And she never stops talking on her phone! She loves going to clubs, too – but it's not my favorite thing! It's probably a bit boring to go out with your father. So it's great that Mariella plays golf with me. It's very special.

Mariella loves bike riding, so we also go bike riding together three times a month. Mariella always decides where to go. Sometimes we take our bikes to the beach, and sometimes to the hills. We often talk – usually about things like school or work. Sometimes we talk about our favorite music. I'm happy to do Mariella's hobby with her. But I hope she never asks me to go shopping with her. I hate going shopping!

Home and away

4A — **LANGUAGE**

GRAMMAR: Prepositions of time

1 Complete the sentences with the words in the box.

> in (x2)   on (x3)   to   at   from

1 _____ Friday nights, I usually get takeout.
2 The bank is open _____ 10 a.m. to 4 p.m.
3 School is always closed _____ August.
4 _____ the winter, I don't go out very often.
5 We study a lot _____ the weekend.
6 I'm always tired _____ Monday mornings.
7 Where were you _____ midnight last night?
8 The outdoor swimming pool is open from May _____ October.

2 Complete the text with prepositions of time.

A typical day? Well, I usually get up ¹_____ 7 a.m., but ²_____ the summer it's lighter, so I get up earlier – maybe 6:30 a.m. I have a job in a café – I serve food to customers.
I work ³_____ 10 a.m. ⁴_____ 6 p.m. every day during the week – ⁵_____ Monday ⁶_____ Friday. After work, ⁷_____ 6 p.m., I usually meet my friends. ⁸_____ Friday nights, we go to a restaurant or to the movies. ⁹_____ July, the café is closed for one month, so I don't work at all. It's also closed ¹⁰_____ New Year's. Then, my typical day is very different!

VOCABULARY: Daily routine verbs

3 Put verbs a–g in order (1–8) to make a typical day.

a get home _____
b finish work _____
c have dinner _____
d go to bed _____
e have breakfast _____
f go to sleep _____
g get up _____
h go to work _____

4 Order the letters to make daily routine verbs.

1 I **egt deserds** after a big breakfast.
2 Do you watch TV before you **og ot loshoc**?
3 My brother often doesn't **veah clunh** because he's busy.
4 Yolanda likes to **kwae pu** early and read a magazine.
5 On Sunday, before I **teg pu**, I have a cup of coffee.
6 Does he **akte a roshew** every morning?
7 Our mom sometimes **saket a hatb** before bed.
8 When they **hsifni closho**, they play in the park.

PRONUNCIATION: Sentence stress

5 ▶ 4.1 Read the sentences. Which words are stressed? Listen, check, and repeat.

1 I get up at eleven o'clock.
2 I go to school from nine o'clock to three o'clock.
3 We have breakfast at 7:30.
4 He rides his bike to work in the summer.
5 I play soccer on Saturday afternoons.
6 She wakes up at eight.

LISTENING: Listening for the main idea

1 ▶4.2 Listen to a conversation about Hong Kong. Check (✔) the different types of weather you hear.

a _____

b _____

c _____

d _____

e _____

f _____

2 ▶4.2 Listen again. Are the sentences true (T) or false (F)?

1 The weather is always the same in Hong Kong. _____
2 Fiona doesn't like hot weather. _____
3 Fiona is a student. _____
4 It never rains in Hong Kong. _____
5 Typhoons bring bad weather. _____

3 Complete the weather words for a–f in exercise 1.

a s_____g
b s_____y
c r_____g
d f_____y
e w_____y
f c_____y

4 Order the letters to make seasons. Which words from exercise 3 describe the weather in your country in each season?

1 RETWIN _____
2 GRINPS _____
3 LALF _____
4 REMUMS _____

5 ▶4.3 Read the sentences. <u>Underline</u> the words which you think will be stressed. Listen and check.

1 What's the climate like there?
2 There are four seasons.
3 The weather is too hot for me.
4 It always rains here!
5 Is Hong Kong a beautiful city?

GRAMMAR: Present continuous

1 Choose the correct options to complete the sentences.

1 I _____ a great time in New York.
   a has   **b** having   **c** 'm having

2 "Where's Peter?" "He _____ his mother right now."
   a 's helping   **b** helps   **c** are helping

3 "Are we eating lunch here?" "No, we _____."
   a don't   **b** 're not   **c** 's not

4 Where _____ you going right now?
   a is   **b** are   **c** do

5 I'm _____ enjoying this movie.
   a doesn't   **b** not   **c** no

6 Are you _____ to the party on Friday?
   a come   **b** comes   **c** coming

7 Laila's _____ tonight, so she's not here.
   a work   **b** works   **c** working

8 _____ they having a karate class today?
   a Do   **b** Are   **c** Is

9 "Is he listening to the radio?" "No, he _____."
   a is   **b** doesn't   **c** 's not

10 They _____ going to clubs downtown this week.
   a 're not   **b** not   **c** don't

2 Order the words to make statements and questions.

1 in / we / the classroom / sitting / are / now
_____.

2 their vacation / Brazil / aren't / they / spending / in
_____.

3 today / are / enjoying / the children / school
_____?

4 she / right now / listening / 's not
_____.

5 visiting / you / this week / are / new places
_____?

6 right / is / now / snowing / it
_____?

7 walking / today / not / the dog / I'm
_____.

8 camping / he / is / this year / going
_____.

PRONUNCIATION: Linking consonants and vowels

3 ▶ 4.4 <u>Underline</u> the words that are linked. Listen, check, and repeat.

1 What are you doing tomorrow?
2 I'm going away next weekend.
3 She's eating her breakfast.
4 It's not very warm today.
5 I'm getting up late tomorrow.
6 He's asking his teacher.

4 Write sentences to describe what the people (1–8) in the picture are doing.

WRITING: Describing a photo

○ ○ ○

Hey Rob,

How are you? I'm having a great time in London. I'm going to summer school – I love learning English! The weather's not very hot, and it rains a lot, but ¹_____'s good weather for learning and sightseeing.

I'm really busy – there's so much to do! Classes start at 9 a.m. and ²_____ finish at 1 p.m. I usually get up early and go for a walk before breakfast. I study English with the other students all morning, and then ³_____ stop for lunch. After lunch, we all go downtown to see the sights. In the evening, we have dinner together. Then we go to the park or play soccer.

I'm sending you a few photos. In this photo, I'm playing soccer with my new friend, George. George is from Serbia – ⁴_____'s really good at sports. This is a photo of my classroom with my English teacher, Joanna. ⁵_____'s really funny, and I enjoy her classes. Here's a photo of my classmates in the park – ⁶_____'s a beautiful place to relax.

Are you in London right now? Can we meet some afternoon?

See you soon,

Fernando

1 Read Fernando's e-mail. Complete 1–6 with the correct pronouns.

2 Number a–e in the order Fernando does the things (1–5).

a describes his daily routine _____
b asks Rob to meet him _____
c talks about the weather _____
d describes some photographs _____
e asks Rob a friendly question _____

3 Complete the sentences with the correct words.

1 In _____ photo, we're playing in the park.
2 This photo is _____ my friend George.
3 _____ is a photo of my teacher, Joanna.
4 _____ this photo, we're having lunch.
5 Here's _____ photo of London.
6 This photo _____ of the other students in my class.

4 You are at a sports camp. Write an e-mail to a friend. Use personal pronouns to avoid repeating words and names.

Talk about:
• the weather
• your daily routine
• some photos and what you are doing in them.

23

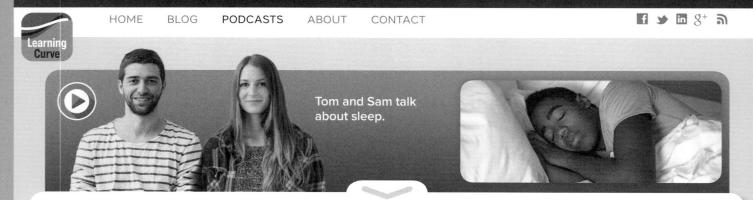

HOME   BLOG   PODCASTS   ABOUT   CONTACT

Tom and Sam talk about sleep.

LISTENING

1 ▶ 4.5 Listen to the podcast about sleep. Check (✓) the things Dr. Patel talks about.

a using a computer   ____
b lunch   ____
c doing yoga   ____
d teenagers   ____
e taking a bath   ____
f taking a shower   ____
g watching TV   ____
h breakfast   ____

2 ▶ 4.5 Listen again. Does Dr. Patel say the things below? Choose Yes or No.

1 Most teenagers don't get enough sleep.	Yes	No
2 Most teenagers need eight hours sleep a night.	Yes	No
3 Dr. Patel eats a big lunch.	Yes	No
4 Dr. Patel has dinner late at night.	Yes	No
5 He takes a bath every evening.	Yes	No
6 He goes to bed after eleven o'clock.	Yes	No
7 He only works on his computer until six o'clock.	Yes	No
8 The light from your phone can stop you from relaxing.	Yes	No

READING

1 Read the blog on page 25 about the weather in two different countries. Match headings 1–5 with paragraphs A–E.

1 Different weather, different clothes   ____
2 Making new friends in a new country   ____
3 Sports at home and away   ____
4 Different lives in two countries   ____
5 Summer and winter weather   ____

2 Check (✓) the true sentences.

1 Patrice is a student from Canada.   ____
2 In Australia, you can swim in the sea in January.   ____
3 He thinks life in Australia is similar to life in Canada.   ____
4 He's wearing warm clothes today.   ____
5 He hates the winter in Canada.   ____
6 The weather in Canada is very different in the summer and winter.   ____
7 Patrice doesn't have many friends in Australia.   ____
8 He never goes surfing in Canada.   ____

3 Circle the weather and seasons vocabulary in the blog.

HOME   BLOG   PODCASTS   ABOUT   CONTACT

Guest blogger Marc writes about the weather in different countries.

NORTH AND SOUTH

What's the weather like in your country? Do you think the weather changes how you feel? What happens when people move from a hot country to a cold country, or from a cold place to somewhere really hot? Twenty-year-old Patrice Chiffre told me about moving from Canada to Australia.

A I come from Calgary, a city in Canada, but now I'm going to college in Australia. The weather in these countries isn't the same at all! And I think it changes how people live and work in these places.

B First, the months and seasons aren't the same. In December in Canada, people wear warm coats and hats, and sometimes have dinner next to a big fire. But in Australia, January is summer and July is winter. Today is the beginning of February, and everyone is wearing T-shirts and shorts. I'm eating lunch by the sea with my friends, and we're enjoying the sunny weather! People often spend New Year's at the beach here.

C Where I'm living in Australia right now, there is a wet season and a dry season. The wet season is really hot, and the dry season is a little colder. But at home in Canada, the winters are long, dark, and really cold. The short and sunny summers bring a big change, so people often eat healthier food, get more exercise, and get up early in the morning. I love the summers in Canada – they are full of energy, festivals, and parties!

D People spend a lot of time outside in Australia, so it's easy to meet people and make new friends. Of course, it's different in Canada, especially in winter. People stay inside more and don't see their friends very often. I'm meeting lots of new people here in Australia!

E One thing I love about Canada is all the snow and ice we have in winter. I love going skiing, too. It hardly ever snows here in Australia, but I enjoy going surfing – that's something I can't do at home!

What are you wearing?

5A LANGUAGE

GRAMMAR: Simple present and present continuous

1 Choose the correct options to complete the sentences.

1 Ramona is Spanish. She *is coming from / comes from* Spain.

2 My aunt *doesn't work / isn't working* near her home.

3 *I eat / I'm eating* a big breakfast every morning.

4 "Where is Katia?" "There she is. *She's wearing / She wears* a blue jacket."

5 Hello! *Are you looking / Do you look* for me?

6 We *don't visit / aren't visiting* our grandparents very often.

7 *Is he watching / Does he watch* TV right now?

8 They *aren't selling / don't sell* magazines in this store.

2 Complete the conversation with the simple present or present continuous form of the verbs in parentheses.

Andy Hi! I'm Andy. ¹ _____ (you/ have) a good time?

Mara Yes, it's a great party! My name's Mara.

Andy Hi Mara! Where ² _____ (you/come from)?

Mara I'm from Brazil, but I ³ _____ (study) in here in Chicago this summer. What about you?

Andy I'm from Boston, but I ⁴ _____ (not live) there right now. I ⁵ _____ (work) here with my parents for a few months.

Mara That's interesting! What ⁶ _____ (they/do)?

Andy They ⁷ _____ (fix) cars. We ⁸ _____ (not make) a lot of money, but my mom ⁹ _____ (enjoy) working with the family!

Mara That's fantastic! My mom ¹⁰ _____ (not have) a job right now, but she wants to be a singer!

VOCABULARY: Clothes and ordinal numbers

3 Match definitions 1–8 with clothes a–h.

1 You might wear these on your legs at the beach. _____

2 This makes your neck warm on a cold day. _____

3 You can put these on your hands when it's cold. _____

4 Men often wear this at work. _____

5 You need these on your feet in the snow. _____

6 You can wear this on your head in summer or winter. _____

7 You wear this around the top of your pants. _____

8 When it's hot and sunny, people wear these on their feet. _____

   a sandals

   b belt

   c hat

   d gloves

   e scarf

   f shorts

   g tie

   h boots

4 Write the words next to the ordinal numbers.

1 11th _____

2 3rd _____

3 12th _____

4 29th _____

5 40th _____

6 36th _____

7 28th _____

8 19th _____

9 31st _____

10 14th _____

PRONUNCIATION: Dates

5 ▶5.1 Underline the stressed words. Listen, check, and repeat.

1 It's May fifteenth.

2 It's December sixth.

3 It's the thirtieth of November.

4 It's April eleventh.

5 It's October twelfth.

6 It's the twenty-third of June.

7 It's the sixteenth of February.

8 It's July twenty-ninth.

9 It's the fourteenth of January.

10 It's August thirty-first.

READING: Identifying facts and opinions

ALL ABOUT CLOTHES ...

I'm Marta, and I'm a fashion blogger from Chile. I love making my own clothes and posting pictures of them on this blog!

A I write my blog at home. I need to wear warm clothes because my house is cold. In this picture, I'm wearing my favorite work clothes – I call this my uniform! I think this dress is [1]*anfcitsat* – it's really long, and it keeps me warm, too. My best friend makes jewelry – in this picture, I'm wearing one of her necklaces.

B I love walking, and there are lots of mountains in Chile. I often go hiking on the weekend. Here I am in my favorite hat and hiking pants. I think they're [2]*tearg*!

C I'm not just a fashion blogger! I also have a part-time job. I work as a waitress in a café near my home. I can wear what I like because there's no uniform. I usually wear this black skirt and attractive white top because I think it looks really [3]*cnei*. Do you like my shoes?

D This is my [4]*eautfilub* little brother! He's only five years old. I really like making clothes for him. He's wearing green pants and a T-shirt because these are his favorite clothes.

E The clothes I make aren't always good. This dress is horrible – it's [5]*sranibregams*! It's too big for me, and it's also too short. It's [6]*fulwa*, I know, but everyone makes mistakes!

1

2

3

4

5

1 Read Marta's blog. Match paragraphs A–E with pictures 1–5.

A _____
B _____
C _____
D _____
E _____

2 Order the letters in words 1–6 in the blog to make adjectives.

1 _____
2 _____
3 _____
4 _____
5 _____
6 _____

3 Read the sentences from some of Marta's other blog posts. Are they opinion (O) or fact (F)?

1 Shopping for clothes is boring. _____
2 There are 25 clothing stores in my town. _____
3 I think that my big brother's clothes are terrible! _____
4 My birthday is on June 23rd. I want to get some new shoes! _____
5 I don't have very nice clothes. _____
6 My mother is a nurse. _____

GRAMMAR: *Can* and *can't*

1 Complete the sentences with *can* or *can't*.

1 I _____ see it because I'm not wearing my glasses.

2 "_____ you help me, please?" "Yes, of course!"

3 "Where is the nearest café?" "I'm sorry, we're not from here. We _____ tell you."

4 Anita is a great photographer. She _____ take really good photos.

5 "Can Miguel cook Chinese food?" "No, he _____."

6 "_____ they speak French?" "Yes, a little."

7 Are you hungry? You _____ have some of my pizza if you want.

8 You _____ buy this book, but you can download it.

9 "Can you see the sea from your house?" "Yes, we _____."

10 She can go to the club tonight, but she _____ stay too late.

2 Complete the sentences with *can* or *can't* and the verbs in the box.

> run   read   teach   come   play   go out
> hear   understand   ask   borrow

1 "_____ I _____ you a question?" "Yes, what is it?"

2 Sarah _____ _____ soccer, but she likes watching it.

3 I'm going to Italy next week. _____ you _____ me some Italian words?

4 "Can you _____ this letter?" "No, I _____. The writing is really small."

5 I _____ _____ very fast because I'm wearing sandals!

6 Alina has a lot of homework, so she _____ _____ tonight.

7 _____ I _____ your book? It looks really interesting.

8 They _____ _____ to my party on Saturday – they're on vacation.

9 "Can you _____ that noise?" "Yes, I _____ – what is it?"

10 I _____ _____ you – you're speaking too fast.

VOCABULARY: Hobbies

3 Match the two parts of the sentences.

1 My friend Anita makes ____
2 Our grandmother collects ____
3 His English teacher plays ____
4 Her sister takes ____
5 What does he draw ____
6 Can you bake ____

a pictures of?
b really good photos of animals.
c a cake for my birthday?
d jewelry like bracelets and necklaces.
e coins. She has over a thousand!
f the drums in a band.

4 Complete the sentences with the correct verbs.

1 At school, we _____ blogs about what we are learning.

2 Daniel _____ pictures of his girlfriend in beautiful colors.

3 My sister _____ online games for hours.

4 Can you _____ chess? Do you want to learn?

5 Costa's aunt wants to _____ him a sweater for the winter.

6 Not many people _____ stamps these days.

PRONUNCIATION: *Can* and *can't*

5 ▶5.2 Say the sentences. How do we say *can* and *can't*? Listen, check, and repeat.

1 I can't sew clothes. Can you?
2 "Can you speak Chinese?" "Yes, I can."
3 John can't sing, but he can play the drums.
4 My mom can cook really well.
5 I can dance, but I can't sing.
6 My dad can leave work early this week.
7 "Can your brother play the violin?" "No, he can't."
8 You can't buy a new top today.

SPEAKING: Offering help

1 ▶5.3 Listen to Tim talking about shopping for his vacation. Check (✔) the clothes you hear.

a coat _____
b boots _____
c scarf _____
d shirt _____
e gloves _____
f sweater _____
g sandals _____
h shorts _____
i socks _____
j T-shirt _____

2 Complete the questions with the words in the box. Then match them with answers a–f below.

sell   in   colors   pay   changing   much

1 Do you have it _____ blue? _____
2 Do you _____ scarves? _____
3 What _____ are there? _____
4 How _____ is this green one? _____
5 Where are the men's _____ rooms, please? _____
6 Can I _____ with this credit card? _____

a They're all 45 dollars.
b I'll show you.
c We do, yes.
d Just a minute, I'll check. Yes, here you are.
e Certainly, sir.
f We have these in black, red, and green.

3 ▶5.3 Listen and check.

4 ▶5.4 Listen to 5 conversations. What does the salesclerk do? Choose the correct option.

	asks if the customer needs help	says that he/she will do something
1		
2		
3		
4		
5		

5 ▶5.4 Read the conversations. What do you think the salesclerk says? Then listen again and check.

1
Salesclerk   Are you OK? Do you _____ any help?
Customer   Yes – do you sell coats?

2
Salesclerk   Can I help _____?
Customer   Yes, please. How much are these pajamas?

3
Customer   Can I pay with this credit card?
Salesclerk   Just a minute, I'll _____.

4
Customer   Where are the men's changing rooms?
Salesclerk   I'll _____ you where they are.

5
Customer   Do you have this suit in medium?
Salesclerk   _____ me ask someone.

6 ▶5.4 Listen again. Repeat what the salesclerk says.

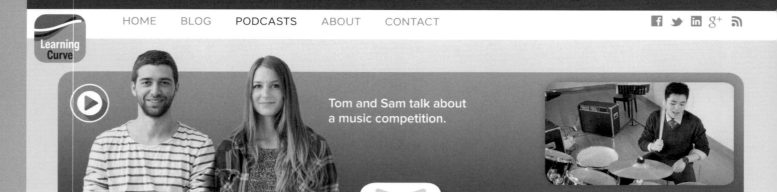

HOME   BLOG   **PODCASTS**   ABOUT   CONTACT

Tom and Sam talk about a music competition.

LISTENING

1 ▶ 5.5 Listen to the podcast about a music competition. Choose the correct answers.

1 How old is Tony Pia?
   a 17
   b 18
   c 20

2 What instrument can Tony play well?
   a the drums
   b the piano
   c the guitar

3 When is the final for the music competition?
   a June 30th
   b January 30th
   c June 13th

2 ▶ 5.5 Listen again. Complete the sentences with one or two words.

1 The competition is called Young Drummer of _____.

2 Young people from all over _____ enter the competition.

3 Tony is feeling a bit _____.

4 Tony's mom can play the _____.

5 Tony plays the drums every _____.

6 Playing the drums makes Tony feel _____ and full of energy.

READING

1 Read the blog on page 31 about what to wear for a job interview. Answer the questions.

1 What is Angela Santo's job?
2 What is Norbert Szil's job?
3 Which person's clothes does Angela prefer?
4 Which person's clothes does Norbert prefer?

2 Are the sentences correct? Choose Yes or No.

1	Angela and Norbert like Jo's hat.	Yes	No
2	Angela doesn't like Jo's scarf.	Yes	No
3	Norbert likes Jo's scarf and top.	Yes	No
4	Norbert thinks Dan looks good.	Yes	No
5	Angela thinks Dan is wearing great clothes for an interview.	Yes	No
6	Angela likes all Isa's clothes.	Yes	No
7	Angela thinks skirts are better than pants for an interview.	Yes	No
8	Norbert thinks Isa's clothes are good for a job in fashion.	Yes	No

3 Circle the clothes vocabulary in the blog.

HOME   **BLOG**   PODCASTS   ABOUT   CONTACT

Guest blogger Ethan hears about wearing the right clothes.

Dress for success

You have an interview for the job of your dreams. Congratulations! So, what are you thinking of wearing on the big day? It can be easy to make bad choices. Angela Santo is a hotel manager, and Norbert Szil has a fashion business. They tell me how to dress for success.

Jo

Angela I'm not at all sure about this one. Why is she wearing a hat? I don't think that hats are a great idea – not for a job interview. And I don't think the scarf is very neat. It looks a little informal, too.

Norbert I agree with Angela about the hat. I don't agree with her about the rest of the clothes, though. This woman is wearing very fashionable clothes, and I think the scarf and top look good together. She looks cool!

Dan

Norbert This man is carrying an old briefcase. It's not at all attractive! It looks awful! I think he's wearing a suit, shirt, and tie, but are those sneakers on his feet? This is never a good look, but for a job interview it's terrible!

Angela I agree with Norbert. This man does not look fashionable. Are you sure he's going to a job interview?

Isa

Angela This woman has it right! The skirt is great – not too long or short – and it's dark blue, which is a great color for interviews. She's wearing a nice jacket, too. Suits are great for interviews, and women can wear pant suits or a skirt and jacket.

Norbert Is this woman looking for a job in a bank? I think she'll do well. There's just one thing – I can't imagine her working in fashion. Her clothes are a bit boring. Some color is always a great thing, and how about some jewelry?

UNIT 6

Homes and cities

GRAMMAR: *there is/there are*, *some/any*, and prepositions of place

1 Complete the text with the words in the box.

> there are   are   are there   there's
> is   any   there   some

So, this is my bedroom – I really like it! ¹_____ a window by my bed, so I can see outside. Across from the bed is a TV. I love watching TV in bed at night! ²_____ some closets, too, for my clothes. ³_____ any shelves? Yes, there ⁴_____ – look! There are ⁵_____ shelves next to the bed. There aren't ⁶_____ books on them because I don't like reading. ⁷_____ are lots of DVDs, though. And ⁸_____ there a desk? No, I do my homework downstairs on the big table!

2 Choose the preposition which is **not** correct.

1 The boy is *in front of / behind / between* the door.
2 The table is *next to / across from / in* a small window.
3 The big chair is *on / behind / in front of* the closet.
4 Is his book *under / between / next to* your shopping bag?
5 My house is *between / under / across from* the park and the station.
6 Two apples are *in / under / on* the table.
7 Your cat is *behind / on / between* the sofa.
8 Is your apartment *next to / between / on* those two stores?
9 Our teacher is *in / next to / in front of* the big desk.
10 Her phone is *behind / in / under* the TV.

VOCABULARY: Rooms and furniture

3 Order the letters to make words for rooms or furniture.

1 Is there a TCLSEO in your bedroom?
_____
2 There are a lot of old books and toys in the TENSMEAB of our house.
_____
3 When it's sunny, I like sitting outside on the YLBCAON.
_____
4 We have got a AGGARE where my parents keep their car.
_____
5 Julia's in the THRABOMO. She's taking a shower.
_____
6 Their house has a OMORDEB upstairs, and one downstairs.
_____

4 Write the words for the definitions.

1 You look at your face in this.
m_____
2 You can wash your clothes in this.
w_____ m_____
3 This is a room at the top of a house.
a_____
4 You walk up and down these.
s_____
5 You eat food here.
d_____ r_____
6 There's grass and sometimes flowers and trees here.
b_____
7 You can do your homework here.
s_____
8 You cook food here.
k_____

PRONUNCIATION: *there's/there are*

5 ▶ 6.1 Say the sentences. How do we say *there's* and *there are*? Listen again and repeat.

1 There's a bed in the living room.
2 There are some chairs next to the table.
3 Is there a sofa in your bedroom?
4 Are there any shelves? No, there aren't.
5 There are five tables in their house.
6 Is there any food in the cabinet?
7 There's a stove in the kitchen.
8 There's no hall in his apartment.

LISTENING: Identifying key points

1 ▶ 6.2 Listen to a TV show about houses. Check (✔) the key points the speakers talk about.

a the furniture ____

b the colors of the rooms ____

c spending time with the family ____

d the backyard ____

e the size of the house ____

2 ▶ 6.2 Listen again. Complete the sentences.

1 The windows are really big and _____.

2 At first, the house had two _____.

3 Loretta has _____ children.

4 The host thinks their furniture is really _____.

5 Loretta's husband really likes _____ furniture.

6 Loretta painted the bathroom and _____.

7 The furniture was _____ expensive.

8 Loretta loves sitting on the _____ in the summer.

3 Read the sentences. Write the full form or contracted form of the underlined words.

1 <u>He's</u> very busy at work. _____

2 <u>There is</u> a picture on the wall. _____

3 The <u>table is</u> near the window. _____

4 <u>It's</u> a sunny day today. _____

5 I <u>do not</u> like vegetables. _____

6 <u>I'm</u> nineteen years old. _____

7 <u>She is</u> not very friendly. _____

8 <u>They're</u> not cheap at all. _____

4 Put the adjectives in the box into seven pairs of opposite meanings.

clean   light   narrow   uncomfortable   dirty
cheap   modern   quiet   heavy   expensive
traditional   wide   noisy   comfortable

1 _____ _____

2 _____ _____

3 _____ _____

4 _____ _____

5 _____ _____

6 _____ _____

7 _____ _____

GRAMMAR: Modifiers

1 Choose the correct options to complete the sentences.

1 I love Suzy's house! It's _____ beautiful.
   a pretty   **b** really   **c** not very
2 I don't like that dress – it's _____ attractive.
   a pretty   **b** not at all   **c** very
3 "Do you like this music?" "It's _____ good, but it's not my favorite."
   a not very   **b** not at all   **c** pretty
4 We don't want any dinner, thanks. We're _____ hungry.
   a really   **b** not very   **c** very
5 Everyone likes Laura. She's _____ friendly.
   a not very   **b** really   **c** pretty
6 "Can you clean your bedroom? It's _____ messy."
   a not at all   **b** not very   **c** really
7 "Can they speak English well?" "They can speak it _____ well, but they want to get better."
   a very   **b** not at all   **c** pretty
8 She's _____ good at sports. She often wins competitions!
   a not at all   **b** not very   **c** very

2 Order the words to make sentences.

1 sunny / not / today / it's / very
2 pretty / good student / is / Emile / a
3 really / costumes / your / colorful / are
4 friendly / her uncle / very / is / not
5 goes / early / to bed / Paola / very
6 not / my / warm / are / gloves / very

VOCABULARY: Places in a city

3 Order the letters to make words for places in a city.

1 QUESOM
2 TREHEAT
3 METNUNOM
4 HETACLADR
5 QERUAS
6 TRAPATEMN DIGLIBUN
7 RGEBID
8 NORETCC LALH

4 Complete the words.

1 My mom goes to the m_____t every morning to buy fruit and vegetables.
2 We live in an old city, so there aren't many s_____s or other tall buildings.
3 My sister loves reading. She's always at the l_____y.
4 There's a small s_____m here. There's a basketball game every weekend.
5 His brother-in-law's an accountant. He works in an o_____e b_____g.
6 In my village, there's a b_____e over the river.

PRONUNCIATION: Sentence stress

5 ▶6.3 Underline the stressed words in the sentences. Listen, check, and repeat.

1 That chair's not very comfortable.
2 Her grandparents' house is pretty modern.
3 It's a very famous painting.
4 That restaurant's not at all expensive.
5 Our balcony is always really sunny.
6 This is a pretty heavy table.
7 The restaurant is very traditional.

WRITING: Topic sentences

A _____ It's on the River Guadalquivir, but it's pretty far from the sea. It's a busy and lively place with a population of 700,000.

B _____ You can visit museums, art centers, theaters, and movie theaters. The Plaza de España is a very famous place. It was built in 1928 and is really popular with tourists. If you like being active, you can play soccer or golf at the parks and sports centers. There are lots of great places to go walking, too.

C _____ There are really fantastic restaurants where you can get delicious tapas and traditional Spanish food. You have to try the delicious potato omelet – it's fantastic!

D _____ A lot of tourists come to the April Fair every spring. This celebration takes place next to the river – it's a wonderful party. There is horseback riding, music, and women wearing colorful flamenco dresses.

E _____ Nicer times to visit are spring and fall, when it's sunny and a little bit cooler.

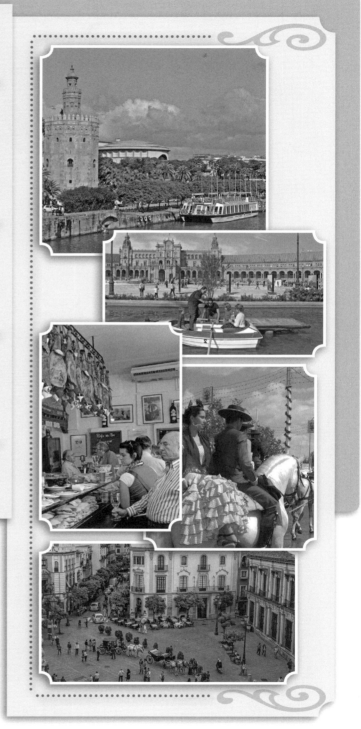

1 Read the text about Seville. Match paragraphs A–E with topic sentences 1–5.

1 If you visit Seville in the summer, it can be very hot. _____

2 Seville is also well known for its festivals. _____

3 You can always find something good to eat in this city. _____

4 Seville is a famous Spanish city. _____

5 There are so many things for tourists to see and do in Seville. _____

2 Complete each sentence about Rome with one word.

1 Rome is the _____ city of Italy.

2 More than 2.5 million people _____ there.

3 Walking is a great _____ to see the sights.

4 There are wonderful _____ of the city from the top of the Gianicolo hill.

5 If _____ like historic sights, go to the Colosseum.

6 There are also lots of really good _____ to eat.

3 Write about a city you know well. Begin each paragraph with a topic sentence. Include the following information:

Paragraph 1: Where is the city?

Paragraph 2: What can you do there?

Paragraph 3: What special events or festivals are there?

Paragraph 4: Where can you go to eat?

Paragraph 5: When is the best time to visit?

HOME   BLOG   **PODCASTS**   ABOUT   CONTACT

Tom and Sam talk about Sally and José's house.

LISTENING

1 ▶ 6.4 Listen to the podcast about Sally and José's house. What is unusual about it?

a   There is no furniture.
b   There are two houses inside it.
c   It's not very neat.

2 ▶ 6.4 Listen again. Are the sentences true (T) or false (F)?

1   Sally and José live in the country.   _____
2   They don't like each other.   _____
3   They can't live together.   _____
4   Sally goes to bed late.   _____
5   José gets up early.   _____
6   They are both clean and tidy.   _____
7   They have the same rooms.   _____
8   José doesn't see Sally every day.   _____

3 ▶ 6.4 Listen again and check (✔) the parts of the house that Sally and José mention.

1   backyard   _____
2   dining room   _____
3   kitchen   _____
4   living room   _____
5   bedroom   _____
6   bathroom   _____
7   basement   _____
8   hall   _____

READING

1 Read the blog on page 37 about Buenos Aires. Match paragraphs A–E with pictures 1–5.

1   _____
2   _____
3   _____
4   _____
5   _____

2 Choose the correct options to complete the sentences.

1   El Ateneo Grand Splendid doesn't sell
    a   books.
    b   furniture.
    c   food and drink.

2   You can watch sports at
    a   San Telmo.
    b   La Poesía.
    c   La Bombonera.

3   You don't have to pay for
    a   the soccer games.
    b   the walking tours.
    c   the coffee at La Poesía.

4   They sell cheap clothes
    a   in the park.
    b   next to the theater.
    c   at the market.

5   San Telmo has lots of
    a   interesting buildings.
    b   good places for music.
    c   parks.

6   The street art tour
    a   is in one part of the city.
    b   is in different parts of the city.
    c   starts next to an ice cream shop.

HOME   **BLOG**   PODCASTS   ABOUT   CONTACT

Tom and Sam write about Buenos Aires.

The best of **Buenos Aires**

We asked our readers to tell us about their favorite places in the beautiful city of Buenos Aires. Thanks for all your great ideas. We want to go there – now! We hope you do, too, when you read our blog!

A   El Ateneo Grand Splendid

El Ateneo Grand Splendid is the best bookshop in the world! It's in a beautiful building, which is nearly a hundred years old. There are lots of books, balconies, and comfortable chairs, and there's a café that sells excellent coffee and delicious pastries. It's perfect for book lovers!

B   La Bombonera

Above the houses and stores of La Boca, you can find the soccer stadium. This is where the Boca junior soccer team plays. It's not too expensive to get a ticket for a game, and it's a really exciting place to spend some time.

C   City walking tours

Every day there are free walking tours of Buenos Aires, and you can choose to see the city during the day or at night. You'll visit modern and traditional buildings, from libraries to cathedrals. There is also a stop at the local market where you can buy clothes and food – clothes are not at all expensive here. The tour begins at the park across from the National Theater and finishes at a bar where you can hear some live Argentinian music.

D   San Telmo

San Telmo is the oldest part of the city. There are narrow streets full of interesting stores, monuments, and some excellent restaurants, too. It's a great place to find an outdoor café, order coffee, and watch the world go by. A very popular café is La Poesía. It's next to a beautiful old church.

E   Street art tour

Buenos Aires is famous for street art, and there are some really colorful paintings. The street art tour is a good way to learn about the artists in this amazing place. It takes you all over the city and finishes in a famous ice cream shop. The guides are really friendly, too!

Our next blog post is about Egypt. Do you have any useful travel tips? Let us know!

Food and drink

7A — LANGUAGE

GRAMMAR: Countable and uncountable nouns + *some/any*

1 Are the nouns countable (C) or uncountable (U)?

1	cheese	C U	6	jewelry	C U
2	salt	C U	7	teacher	C U
3	library	C U	8	mirror	C U
4	bread	C U	9	pasta	C U
5	lemonade	C U	10	sofa	C U

2 Complete the sentences with *some* or *any*.

1 Is there _____ coffee in the cabinet?

2 I'd like _____ yogurt.

3 There isn't _____ tea here – can you buy some?

4 Can I have _____ onions? I need them to make lunch.

5 She usually has _____ fruit after dinner.

6 Would you like _____ tomato soup?

7 Are there _____ lemons in the kitchen?

8 I don't want _____ water.

VOCABULARY: Food and drink

3 Complete the conversation with the words in the box. There are two extra words.

> juice   ice cream   cookies   tea   potatoes
> cake   peas   cereal   orange   mushroom

Miguel Peter's coming to dinner tonight.

Eva Great! I can make some
¹_____ soup. I know he likes it.

Miguel We have some fish. Do we have any
²_____? I can make some French fries. We can have some
³_____, too.

Eva That sounds good! What about drinks? Do we need any ⁴_____?

Miguel Yes, Peter's favorite is
⁵_____.

Eva OK. Now we need something for dessert. ⁶_____ ?

Miguel No, it's too cold! Why don't you get a
⁷_____ ?

Eva Great idea! And after that, we can have
⁸_____ or coffee.

4 Write the words for definitions 1–8. Then match 1–8 with pictures a–h.

1 a long green vegetable   c_____

2 a small round red fruit   s_____

3 you eat this in hot weather   i___ c_____

4 a long yellow fruit   b_____

5 a long orange vegetable   c_____

6 a large round green vegetable   c_____

7 a small round fruit, sometimes green   g_____

8 a round yellow fruit   l_____

PRONUNCIATION: *some/any*

5 ▶ 7.1 Say the sentences. Are *some* and *any* stressed? Listen, check, and repeat.

1 There are some bananas on the table.

2 Is there any milk in the fridge?

3 She's buying some strawberries at the market.

4 I don't want any cookies, thanks.

5 There isn't any pepper.

6 I'd like some potato chips with my lunch.

READING: Skimming a text

BREAKFAST AROUND THE WORLD!

Breakfast is the most important meal of the day because it gives us the energy we need to work and learn. In many European countries, the first meal of the day is a piece of bread and some coffee. In other countries, people eat much more. So, what exactly do people around the world have for breakfast?

Paulo, Brazil:

I have breakfast with my family – we sit together and talk about the day ahead. We usually have coffee and some bread with cheese. We also like to have some fruit – it's delicious!

Jason, Australia:

In Australia, we have lots of excellent seasonal fruit, so it's a popular breakfast. I'm too busy to cook in the morning, so I often have an apple and some yogurt. Sometimes I don't even have enough time to eat that, so I take the yogurt to work with me.

Jenny, Ireland:

I leave home early, so I rarely eat anything. I usually just have a cup of tea. I know it's really unhealthy! On weekends, I have more time – so I have an egg sandwich.

Asil, Turkey:

My mom always makes my breakfast – she's an excellent cook. I usually have some bread, cheese, eggs, and tomatoes – that's a popular breakfast in Turkey.

Yoko, Japan:

For breakfast, I often have rice and vegetables. I like miso soup, too. It is a very popular breakfast in Japan. I sometimes have that because it's a healthy breakfast. It gives me energy to study when I'm in school.

1 Skim the text. Answer the questions with one word.

1 Many European people drink coffee for _____.
2 Brazilians often have bread with _____.
3 _____ is a popular breakfast in Australia.
4 Jenny usually has a cup of _____ for breakfast.
5 Asil's _____ is a really good cook.
6 People in _____ eat miso soup.

2 Choose the correct options to answer the questions.

1 Breakfast is important because
   a it gives you energy for the day.
   b you eat it with your family.
   c it helps you sleep better.

2 Paulo eats his first meal of the day
   a alone.
   b with his family.
   c with his friends.

3 Why doesn't Jenny eat breakfast?
   a She thinks it's unhealthy.
   b She's too busy.
   c She doesn't have enough money.

4 Jenny eats egg sandwiches
   a for lunch.
   b on Saturdays and Sundays.
   c every day.

5 In Turkey, a lot of people
   a don't eat breakfast.
   b eat the same breakfast as Asil.
   c drink tea for breakfast.

6 Yoko
   a has breakfast in school.
   b rarely eats miso soup.
   c doesn't eat the same breakfast every day.

3 Choose the correct options to complete the sentences.

1 Paulo eats breakfast with his family. *He / They / We* sit and talk about the day ahead.

2 Jason doesn't have time to eat breakfast. *His / Its / Their* morning is just too busy!

3 I love eggs. *It's / My / Their* favorite breakfast is an egg sandwich.

4 Fruit is really good in Australia. *Its / It's / It* a popular breakfast.

5 Asil's mother makes his breakfast. *She / Her / He* is an excellent cook.

6 Yoko thinks breakfast is important. *They / It / She* gives her energy to study when she's in school.

7 Most of us eat breakfast, but *you / we / it* eat different things in different countries.

8 We usually go out for lunch on a Sunday. *Your / Its / Our* favorite restaurant is Gino's.

GRAMMAR: Quantifiers: *(how) much, (how) many, a lot of, a few, a little*

1 Choose the correct options to complete the sentences.

1 I'm drinking _____ carrot juice right now. I want to be healthy.

   a much **b** a lot of **c** a few

2 Can I have _____ milk in my coffee, please?

   a many **b** a few **c** a little

3 How _____ meals do you usually eat?

   a many **b** much **c** few

4 Sara eats _____ cakes and cookies. It's not very healthy!

   a a little **b** a few **c** a lot of

5 "Are there any potatoes?" "There are _____."

   a a few **b** a little **c** much

6 Millie usually has _____ cereal for breakfast, but I don't think it's enough.

   a a little **b** a lot of **c** many

7 How _____ meat does he eat every week?

   a much **b** little **c** many

2 Complete the text with the correct quantifiers. Write one word in each space.

People often ask me how to stay healthy. I have a **1**_____ good ideas. First, I always have a big breakfast, so I don't need **2**_____ snacks in the middle of the morning. The people I work with eat a lot **3**_____ cakes and cookies at eleven o'clock – not me! I eat **4**_____ little cake sometimes and a **5**_____ potato chips – but not many. How **6**_____ cola do I drink? None! I drink a **7**_____ coffee, but I drink a **8**_____ of water, too. And how **9**_____ glasses of water do I drink? Probably about seven every day.

VOCABULARY: Containers and portions

3 Match the two parts of the sentences.

1 Could we have a can _____

2 I need a bottle of _____

3 Can you buy a box _____

4 He'd like a bag of _____

5 Is there a bag of _____

6 Laura has a bar _____

7 I often have a bowl _____

   a of chocolate in her desk.

   b water – I'm really thirsty!

   c of pasta for my dinner.

   d potato chips with his lunch.

   e of corn, please?

   f onions in the kitchen?

   g of cereal for breakfast tomorrow?

4 Complete the words.

1 I'm going to the store for a c_____ of milk.

2 "There are no fresh tomatoes." "Why don't you buy some in a c_____?"

3 It's my birthday today! Have a s_____ of cake.

4 My mom has a c_____ of tea every morning.

5 It's really hot! Do you want a g_____ of cold water?

6 There are some olives in that j_____. Would you like some?

7 Have a p_____ of this cheese with your bread.

PRONUNCIATION: Weak form *of*

5 ▶7.2 Say the sentences. How do we say *of*? Listen, check, and repeat.

1 I don't eat a lot of candy.

2 How many cups of coffee do you drink?

3 Do you want a box of cookies?

4 How many glasses of juice do they want?

5 There is a bowl of fruit on the table.

6 Where is the bottle of olive oil?

SPEAKING: Asking politely for something

1 (▶) **7.3** Listen. What do the customers order at the restaurant? Choose the correct information.

1	2	3	4
3 customers Name: Cellini 2 x vegetable soup 1 x steak + French fries 1 x lasagna 2 x mineral water 2 x fruit salad	2 customers Name: Cellini 2 x vegetable soup 1 x steak + French fries 1 x lasagna 2 x mineral water	2 customers Name: Cellini 1 x vegetable soup 1 x lasagna 2 x steak + French fries 2 x mineral water	2 customers Name: Cellini 1 x vegetable soup 1 x lasagna 2 x steak + French fries 2 x mineral water 1 x ice cream

2 (▶) **7.3** Put the lines from the conversation in order. Then listen again and check.

a Are you ready to order your main course? ____

b Can I take your name? ____

c The name's Cellini. ____

d Of course. I'll just go and get it for you. ____

e Would you like anything for dessert? ____

f Could we just have the check, please? ____

g Hello, do you have a table for eight o'clock this evening, please? ____

h We have a table reserved in the name of Cellini. ____

i For how many people? ____

j It's for two people. ____

k Hello, Giovanni's Restaurant. How can I help you? ____

l Can I get you any drinks? ____

m Ah yes, this way, please. ____

n Would you like a starter? ____

3 (▶) **7.4** Complete the sentences for asking politely. Then listen and check.

1 _____ both like the vegetable soup.

2 I'd _____ the steak and French fries, please.

3 _____ I have the lasagna, please?

4 Can I _____ a glass of water, please?

4 Practice saying the sentences in exercise 3. Make sure you use polite intonation.

5 Reply to the waiter's questions. Use the information in parentheses.

1 Hello, Moonlight Restaurant. How can I help? (you/table/three people?)

2 Good evening, sir. Can I help you? (have/reserved/name/Smith)

3 Would you like a starter? (like/chicken soup)

4 Are you ready to order your main course? (can/have/large salad?)

5 What would you like to drink? (could/have/apple juice?)

6 Can I help you? (we/have/check?)

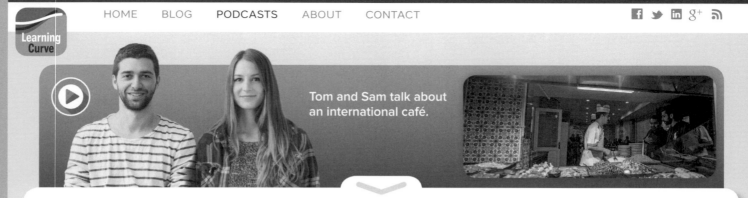

HOME   BLOG   **PODCASTS**   ABOUT   CONTACT

Tom and Sam talk about an international café.

LISTENING

1 ▶ 7.5 Listen to the podcast about an international café. Number a–f in the order you hear them (1–6).

a peppers _____
b cheese _____
c rice _____
d tomatoes _____
e cake _____
f chicken _____

2 ▶ 7.5 Listen again. Are the sentences true (T) or false (F)?

1 Gabriela Romero is the manager of the international café. _____
2 People of different nationalities cook American food in the café. _____
3 The money from the café goes to charity. _____
4 Gabriela started the café alone. _____

3 ▶ 7.5 Listen again. Complete the sentences with one or two words.

1 Gabriela is from _____.
2 Gabriela lives in _____ now.
3 She made _____ burritos for her friends.
4 It costs $_____ to eat at the café.
5 Gabriela is making _____ for dinner.
6 The Turkish chef is making a big bowl of _____ pudding.

READING

1 Read the blog on page 43 about eating local food. Check (✓) the things Alex eats during the five days he describes.

a mushrooms _____
b orange juice _____
c beans _____
d carrots _____
e cola _____
f tomatoes _____
g onions _____
h cabbage _____
i potatoes _____
j eggs _____

2 Choose the correct answers.

1 Why doesn't he eat a lot of fruit?
   a They don't grow much fruit where he lives.
   b He doesn't really like it.
   c It's very expensive where he lives.

2 How does he feel at the start of the week?
   a He's excited – it's going to be fun.
   b He's not very excited – it won't be fun.
   c He's worried – he can't cook.

3 What does he eat on Day One?
   a nothing
   b porridge
   c supermarket cereal

4 Alex gets the ingredients for his omelet from
   a the supermarket.
   b the local store.
   c his aunt's backyard.

5 What happens when Alex goes to the local store?
   a He doesn't buy the things he planned to buy.
   b He pays too much money.
   c He forgets his shopping.

6 What doesn't Alex eat from his aunt's backyard on Day Five?
   a peppers
   b potatoes
   c cabbage

HOME   BLOG   PODCASTS   ABOUT   CONTACT

Guest blogger Jack writes about eating local food.

Going local

Did you realize that the fruit and vegetables you eat can travel thousands of miles around the world before they reach you – and could be weeks old? That's why many people are trying to eat locally instead. I asked my friend, Alex McKay, from Scotland, to try to eat only local food for five days. Read his diary to find out what happened!

Day One

The weather here is often cold and rainy this time of year. We don't grow much fruit, so I'm not sure if this local only diet is going to be much fun!

For breakfast, I usually have a glass of orange juice and a bowl of supermarket cereal. Not today! I have some porridge from my grandmother (that's a kind of popular cereal in Scotland that's similar to oatmeal) and a cup of tea. The porridge tastes OK, and I find that I like knowing where my breakfast comes from.

Day Two

Today I go fishing in the river near my home. I'm really happy when (after a couple of hours) I catch a fish! I walk back and find a farmers' market selling potatoes and beans. These will make a perfect dinner with my delicious fresh fish!

Day Three

I'm not sure what to eat today. Luckily, my aunt comes to visit. She grows vegetables and she brings me some eggs, mushrooms, and onions. Great – I have the ingredients for an omelet. My aunt stays for dinner, and we eat together. This is much better than supermarket shopping!

Day Four

Today everything goes wrong! I go to the local store to buy some carrots for a healthy soup. But I come out with some cookies, a slice of cake, and two cans of cola. Not a healthy lunch!

Day Five

It's the last day! I cook some tasty stew with cabbage and peppers from my aunt's backyard, so I know they're fresh.

So how do I feel after my week of eating locally? Well, it can get a bit boring at times, but it's super healthy, and it's really good to know where your food comes from. Why not try it yourself?

UNIT 8

In the past

GRAMMAR: Past of *be*, *there was*, *there were*, and simple past: irregular verbs

1 Choose the correct options to complete the sentences.

1 _____ you good at sports when you were young?

   a Were **b** Was **c** Wasn't

2 We had a test yesterday. It _____ really difficult.

   a was **b** weren't **c** were

3 Last year, I visited Rome. It's very beautiful, but it _____ cheap!

   a was **b** were **c** wasn't

4 Why _____ you at the party last night?

   a was **b** wasn't **c** weren't

5 His parents _____ rich, but they had a big house.

   a was **b** were **c** weren't

6 It was a warm day, and there _____ lots of people in town.

   a was **b** were **c** wasn't

2 Complete the sentences with the simple past form of the verbs in parentheses.

Last week, I **1**_____ (be) in New York. I **2**_____ (go) with my family: my mom, aunt, and two brothers. We **3**_____ (have) a really good time. Of course, we **4**_____ (see) all the sights – the Statue of Liberty, Central Park, and Times Square – and I **5**_____ (take) lots of photos. There are some great stores there, so I **6**_____ (buy) lots of new clothes – jeans, sneakers, and tops. We all loved the food, too – we **7**_____ (eat) some fantastic meals. We **8**_____ (come) home on Friday – but I want to go back again very soon!

VOCABULARY: Inventions

3 Complete the sentences with the words in the box.

> digital camera toaster smartphone microwave laptop dishwasher CD player

1 I couldn't live without my _____ in my pocket. I call my friends and play games on it, too!

2 We were late, but Mom left our dinner in the _____.

3 Our _____ is broken – the bread comes out black!

4 Suki's hobby is taking photos – she has a really expensive _____.

5 I don't enjoy washing the dishes after meals. I wish we had a _____.

6 Do your parents still listen to music on a _____?

7 I couldn't do my homework last night. My _____ broke, and I lost all my work!

4 Complete the conversation with the correct words.

Anna	What kinds of things were there in your house when you were young, Grandma?
Grandma	There wasn't a lot of technology in those days. For example, there was a radio, but we only had a black and white **1**_____ to watch in the evenings, and we didn't have a DVD **2**_____.
Anna	Really? And there was no **3**_____ TV?
Grandma	Oh no, only black and white! And we didn't have a fridge or **4**_____ to keep our food cold, and there was no **5**_____ to dry your clothes when you washed them!
Anna	But were you happy?
Grandma	Yes, I was! Life was interesting. We didn't have a **6**_____ in our cars, so when you went somewhere new, you sometimes got lost. That was an adventure!

PRONUNCIATION: *was* and *were*

5 ▶ 8.1 Underline the words you think will be stressed. Then say the sentences. Listen, check, and repeat.

1 My grandmother's life was very interesting.

2 We weren't bored in school yesterday.

3 Her parents were both teachers.

4 There weren't many people in the market.

5 There was a bar of chocolate in the fridge.

6 I wasn't tired when I went to bed.

7 I told the waiter that my French fries were cold.

8 It wasn't very sunny last week.

LISTENING: Listening for numbers, dates, and prices

1 Order the letters to make life stages.

1 EB RONB

_____

2 IFNSHI HLOOCS

_____

3 OG TO LGECLOE

_____

4 TEG REDIRMA

_____

5 EVAH A MAYFIL

_____

6 TGE VDECRODI

_____

7 TIREER

_____

2 ▶8.2 Listen to the description of a woman's life. Write the numbers of the four life stages in exercise 1 that you hear.

_____ _____ _____ _____

3 ▶8.2 Listen again. Complete the sentences with numbers, dates, and prices.

1 Bertha wrote a book when she was _____ years old.
2 Bertha was born in _____.
3 Bertha and Fred had _____ children.
4 The camp was very popular in the _____s.
5 Bertha cooked meals for _____ people every day.
6 People stopped going to the camp in the _____s.
7 Fred died in _____.

4 Write the irregular past forms of the verbs from the audio.

1 begin _____
2 do _____
3 go _____
4 know _____
5 leave _____
6 take _____
7 think _____
8 meet _____

5 Order the words to make set phrases.

1 now / for / bye

_____!

2 of / would / cup / like / coffee / a / you

_____?

3 do / you / do / what

_____?

4 you / of / can / course

_____!

5 just / time / I'm / in

_____.

6 a / tea / cup / of

_____.

7 of / paper / piece / a

_____.

8 all / of / first

_____.

GRAMMAR: Simple past: regular verbs and past time expressions

1 Complete the time expressions with *last*, *ago*, *yesterday*, or *in*.

1 _____ week

2 two days _____

3 _____ 1975

4 _____ afternoon

5 a year _____

6 _____ evening

7 _____ the summer

8 three hours _____

9 _____ night

10 _____ the 21st century

2 Complete the sentences with the simple past form of regular verbs.

1 Where were you yesterday? I w_____ to see you.

2 It was a fantastic party! We d_____ all night.

3 We were friends when we were younger. We p_____ together every day.

4 "Did you have a good trip?" "Yes, I really e_____ it, thanks."

5 We p_____ a big party for Jen's birthday.

6 She s_____ really hard at school – that's why she has a good job now.

7 Sam t_____ to fix my bike, but it was no good – it was broken.

8 Diana o_____ the door and went inside, but no one was there.

3 Complete the conversations. Use the simple past form of the verbs in the box.

| want | use | not study | call | enjoy |
| fail | not save | watch | stop | not like |

1 "What did you do yesterday evening?" "Nothing much. We just _____ TV."

2 "How was your Spanish course?" "Terrible! I _____ so I _____ the exam!"

3 "What did you think of the new boss?" "I really _____ her."

4 "We _____ shopping online last month, but we _____ any money!"

5 "Were you busy last night? I _____ you but there was no answer." "I went swimming with my friend."

6 "How was the film yesterday?" "I really _____ it but Meg hated it!"

7 "Why did Emma leave?" "I think she _____ to get home early."

8 "This soup is horrible!" "Yes, I think I _____ too much salt."

4 Read the text and fill in blanks 1–8 with one word.

I ¹t_____ to Mexico to see my sister, Emma, ²l_____ summer. She met a Mexican man a few years ³_____ and moved to Mexico to marry him ⁴_____ 2015. I had a great time there! I ⁵s_____ in my sister's apartment in Mexico City, and we ⁶v_____ a lot of beautiful and interesting places together. She lives near a lot of good restaurants and cafés. We went out every night and I ⁷d_____ want to come home. ⁸Y_____ evening Emma called me. She wants me to go and visit her again next year!

PRONUNCIATION: *-ed* endings

5 ▶ 8.3 Circle the correct sound for the *-ed* endings. Listen, check, and repeat.

1	We tried to tell you, but you didn't listen.	/t/	/d/	/ɪd/
2	She decided to buy a new smartphone.	/t/	/d/	/ɪd/
3	They traveled across Africa by bicycle.	/t/	/d/	/ɪd/
4	Tom played with his toys in his bedroom.	/t/	/d/	/ɪd/
5	Katia liked reading books and listening to music.	/t/	/d/	/ɪd/
6	He waited all day to see her.	/t/	/d/	/ɪd/
7	Your mom looked very tired today.	/t/	/d/	/ɪd/
8	No one wanted to go to clubs.	/t/	/d/	/ɪd/
9	A police officer stopped the man's car.	/t/	/d/	/ɪd/
10	The bad weather ended in March.	/t/	/d/	/ɪd/

WRITING: Planning and making notes

Last week, my friend Carla invited me on a date for the first time. At first, I was excited, but I didn't have a good day.

1_____, I went to buy Carla some flowers.
2_____ I paid for them, I walked to the movie theater and waited outside. I waited there for almost an hour. When Carla arrived, she said, "Sorry – my phone's not working today!"
I was a bit annoyed, but I didn't say anything. 3_____, we went into the movie theater and watched a movie. Carla laughed a lot. I didn't know why, because it wasn't very funny.
4_____, in the evening, we went to a restaurant. Carla ordered an expensive meal, but I wasn't hungry. We talked about the movie and finished our food. 5_____, Carla looked in her bag and said, "Sorry – I don't have any money with me!"

We said goodbye 6_____ my bus arrived, but I was very tired and unhappy. I don't want to go on a date with Carla again!

1 Read the text about Roberto's day. Look at the pictures and write a–f in the correct order.

1 _____
2 _____
3 _____
4 _____
5 _____
6 _____

2 Read the text again. Fill in the blanks with the words in the box.

after   first   before   then (x2)   later

3 Answer the questions about Roberto's bad day.

1 When did it happen?
_____
2 How did Roberto feel at the start?
_____
3 What were the main events?
_____
4 How did Roberto feel after he said goodbye to Carla?
_____
5 What did Roberto think about Carla at the end?
_____

4 Write about a good or bad day you had. Use sequencers to show the order of events. Use the questions from exercise 3 to help you.

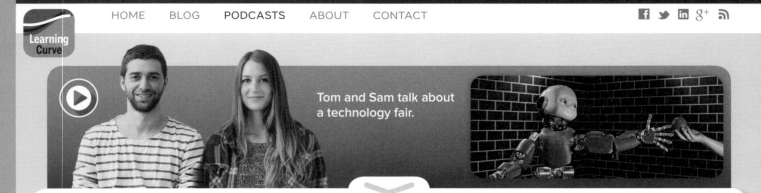

HOME BLOG **PODCASTS** ABOUT CONTACT

Tom and Sam talk about a technology fair.

LISTENING

1 ▶ 8.4 Listen to the podcast about a technology fair. Which three inventions <u>don't</u> you hear?

a digital camera _____
b toaster _____
c smartphone _____
d freezer _____
e microwave _____
f (clothes) dryer _____

2 ▶ 8.4 Listen again. Choose the correct options to complete the sentences.

1 Izumi is *an inventor / a robot*.
2 Daichi is *an inventor / a robot*.
3 The robot can help *students / tourists*.

3 ▶ 8.4 Listen again. Complete the sentences with one or two words.

1 Tom was at the technology fair last _____.
2 Tom didn't buy a robot because it was very _____.
3 Daichi helps to guide people in big cities like _____.
4 The robot can show people how to _____ tickets for the subway.
5 Izumi studied technology _____.
6 It took Izumi _____ to make the robot.

READING

1 Read the blog on page 49 about a famous invention. Are the statements true (T) or false (F)?

1 Ruth Wakefield invented the chocolate chip cookie. _____
2 Ruth knew a lot about food and cooking. _____
3 The cookie's name comes from the name of a hotel. _____
4 She wrote a book about her life. _____
5 At first, Ruth didn't put any chocolate in the cookies. _____
6 When Ruth sold the recipe for the cookies, she made a lot of money. _____

2 Number sentences a–h in the correct order (1–8).

a Ruth got married. _____
b World War II began. _____
c A business bought Ruth's cookie recipe. _____
d Ruth opened a hotel. _____
e Ruth finished school. _____
f Ruth wrote a book about cooking. _____
g Ruth started her first job. _____
h Lots of people wrote to Ruth. _____

HOME   **BLOG**   PODCASTS   ABOUT   CONTACT

Guest blogger Penny writes about an interesting story.

A tasty invention!

You may eat chocolate chip cookies every day, but you probably don't know anything about the woman who invented them! Here's the true story of Ruth Wakefield ...

Ruth Wakefield was born in Massachusetts on June 17, 1903. She probably loved food from a young age because it was very important to her when she was older.

After she finished school, in 1924, she became a dietitian – someone who teaches people about food and how to have a healthy diet. In 1930, she bought a hotel called the Toll House Inn with her husband, Kenneth Donald Wakefield. It was very popular, and visitors came from all over the world. One of the most famous visitors was John F. Kennedy, before he became the president of the U.S. in 1961!

Ruth became famous for her excellent fish dinners and desserts, and in 1930, she wrote a very successful recipe book. Then, Ruth invented the chocolate chip cookie. It became really popular. Some people think that it was an accident and that Ruth wanted the chocolate to melt into the cookie. But the chocolate stayed solid, and that was the start of the cookie we all know and love today! The first recipe for how to make this famous cookie appeared in Ruth's cookbook in 1938.

During the Second World War, families sent chocolate chip cookies to their sons, brothers, and fathers who were soldiers a long way from home. They shared the cookies with other soldiers, and so lots of people tried them and loved them. Ruth started to get hundreds of letters from people who liked her cookies and who wanted more.

In the end, Ruth sold her recipe for Toll House Chocolate Crunch Cookies to a big company. Ruth only got one dollar for the recipe, but she also got a supply of chocolate for her whole life!

Ruth died in 1977 at the age of 73. Next time you bite into one of her delicious cookies, stop and think about the person who invented it!

UNIT 9 Education, education!

GRAMMAR: Simple past: questions

1 Choose the correct options to complete the questions.

1 What subjects *was / did / were* he study in college?
2 *What / Who / Why* was your favorite subject?
3 *What / When / Why* did you do after school?
4 *When / What / Who* was your best friend?
5 *Did / Was / Were* she have a lot of friends in kindergarten?
6 *Who / How / Where* did you eat lunch every day?
7 *Were / Was / Did* there a library in your elementary school?
8 *How / What / Where* did you play sports?
9 *Who / Where / How* was his first teacher in high school?
10 *Was / Did / Were* your teachers good?

2 Complete the conversation with past of *be* or simple past questions.

Sara ¹_____were you yesterday? I called you three times.

Martin I was with Peter.

Sara Really? ²_____ did you do all day?

Martin First we went to the park, and later we played tennis.

Sara And ³_____ did you go after that?

Martin In the evening, we went to the movies.

Sara Ah, you went to the movies?

Martin Yes, I ⁴_____.

Sara ⁵_____ did you go with? Your friend Lisa?

Martin No, I ⁶_____. I told you, I went with Peter! What ⁷_____ you do all day?

Sara Well, I tried to call you. Then I called Peter.

Martin Ah! ⁸_____ he there?

Sara Yes, he ⁹_____. He was home. So, was he with you?

Martin Ah, no. He ¹⁰_____.

VOCABULARY: School subjects and education

3 Complete the text with the words in the box.

elementary   nursery   homework
college   exams   high school

In Scotland, children usually start ¹_____ school when they are three years old. They spend two years there, and then they go to ²_____ school when they are four or five. There they learn to read and write. They don't take ³_____ – they play a lot and learn by doing things. They start ⁴_____ when they are twelve. They work very hard, and have to do more ⁵_____ after school. If they do well, when they finish high school, students can go to ⁶_____ when they are about eighteen.

4 Complete the sentences.

1 I love learning about other countries so my favorite subject is g_____.
2 Ben hates m_____ because he isn't good with numbers.
3 Suki didn't study very hard so she f_____ her exam.
4 Which books are you reading in your l_____ class?
5 My little brother is only five, so he goes to k_____.
6 Victor decided to study l_____. He wants to speak French and Russian.
7 We love sports, so we always enjoy p_____ e_____ class.
8 When I finish school, I want to go to c_____.

PRONUNCIATION: Intonation in questions

5 ▶ 9.1 Read the questions. Do they have rising or falling intonation at the end? Listen, check, and repeat.

1 Did you go to kindergarten?
2 Why didn't you study art?
3 Who was your best friend in school?
4 Was the lesson interesting?
5 Did you have homework on the weekend?

READING: Understanding words that you don't know

Meet three students who found out that it is never too late to learn!

Francisco Pardo

My dad was a self-employed builder. He had his own business and wanted me to go and work with him, **1**_____ I left high school at sixteen. I didn't like working as a builder, though – I was bored, **2**_____ I started looking for something else. I bought a book about computer programming and read it from start to finish. Ten years later (and after a lot more reading and working with computers), I work for a computer company. I absolutely love it!

Bistra Nikolovo

I really liked school, but I thought that when I left college that was the end of learning. Then I discovered online studying. Last year I took courses on Shakespeare, in Italian, and on astronomy – I've always been interested in the stars! This year I'm doing Spanish and film making. I don't want to stop **3**_____ I really enjoy learning this way!

Samantha Jones

I finished school without any real skills **4**_____ I had my daughter when I was eighteen. When she started high school, I found that it was really tough helping her with her math homework. I had to do something about it, **5**_____ I took a night class. My teacher was amazing, and I was really surprised that I could do the work. In the end, I went to college and studied teaching. I'm still doing that now – I work in an elementary school.

1 Read the text and answer each question with a word, a name or a number.

1 What did Francisco study after he left school?
_____

2 What job did Francisco's father want him to do?
_____

3 Who is taking online courses? _____

4 Which language did Bistra study last year?
_____

5 How old was Samantha when she started a family?
_____

6 What is Samantha's job? _____

2 Complete 1–5 in the text with *because* or *so*.

3 Find the words in the text. Are they nouns (N), adjectives (A), or verbs (V)?

1 bored _____
2 discovered _____
3 astronomy _____
4 skills _____
5 tough _____
6 amazing _____

4 Match 1–6 in exercise 3 with meanings a–f.

a something you learn from practice and study _____
b the study of the moon, stars, etc. _____
c not easy, difficult _____
d really good, surprising _____
e found out about _____
f not interested _____

GRAMMAR: Verb patterns: verb + *to* infinitive

1 Complete the text with *to* + the verbs in the box. There are two extra verbs.

> do   travel   move   make
> become   start   get   study

> We're in our last year at school, and we're all planning what we want
> **1**_____ next year. Emile's family want **2**_____ to Australia, so he's going to look for a job there. My friend Roberto hopes **3**_____ a doctor after college. He needs **4**_____ saving some money to pay for his studies. And me? I'm planning **5**_____ English so I can teach it one day. I'd like **6**_____ around the world with this job.

2 Complete the sentences with a *to* infinitive or the *-ing* form of the verbs in parentheses. Some sentences have two answers.

1 Do you like _____ in the sea? (swim)
2 We'd love _____ your new boyfriend! (meet)
3 Jack doesn't like _____ his parents' car. (drive)
4 William is learning _____ Japanese this year. (speak)
5 My uncle offered _____ us to the station. (take)
6 Would you like _____ in our new armchair? (sit)
7 They decided _____ married next year. (get)
8 Will he agree _____ you on Friday evening? (meet)
9 His dog loves _____ with a soccer ball in the park. (play)
10 Did Olivia choose _____ sneakers or sandals? (wear)

VOCABULARY: Resolutions

3 Choose the correct options to complete the text.

> It's a new year and a new you! My name's Penelope Powers, and I'm a life coach. Do you want to get in shape and **1**____ more exercise? I can help you with your goals – and if you want to **2**____ a marathon, I can make it happen! Perhaps you'd like more money? Do you want to **3**____ a car or your dream house? Or maybe you need to **4**____ a new job? I can give you lots of good ideas for when you **5**____ an interview. Of course, relationships are important, too. When you work hard, it's difficult to **6**____ someone new. I can help you **7**____ a relationship or **8**____ new friends. So, if you want to make a new start this year, let me know!

1 **a** be   **b** go   **c** get
2 **a** get   **b** run   **c** have
3 **a** buy   **b** make   **c** save
4 **a** be   **b** get   **c** earn
5 **a** have   **b** make   **c** save
6 **a** make   **b** meet   **c** join
7 **a** improve **b** run   **c** meet
8 **a** be   **b** make   **c** lose

4 Complete the sentences with the correct verbs.

1 Tony really needs to _____ in shape. He drives everywhere and watches too much TV.
2 My boss isn't happy with me. She says I need to _____ more organized.
3 I love my job, but I'd like to _____ more money.
4 You don't need to _____ your diet. You already drink lots of water and eat healthy food.
5 We need to _____ some money if we want to go on vacation to Greece.
6 She wants to _____ weight. Her clothes are too small.
7 Oskar's planning to _____ a gym next month.
8 My sister's a salesclerk, but she wants to _____ a new job as a receptionist.

PRONUNCIATION: *'d like* and *like*

5 ▶9.2 Say the sentences. How do we say *'d like* and *like*? Listen, check, and repeat.

1 I'd like to go downtown this afternoon.
2 They'd like to have a barbecue.
3 We like eating healthy food.
4 I like my new boss.
5 We'd like to speak Spanish.
6 They like staying in shape.

SPEAKING: Sounding sympathetic

1 ▶ 9.3 Listen to the conversation between two friends. Are the statements true (T) or false (F)?

1 Rakeem has a lot of English homework. _____

2 He did badly on an exam. _____

3 He wants to find a part-time job. _____

4 Rakeem needs some extra money. _____

5 He doesn't think it's a good idea to talk to his family. _____

6 He can't sleep because of his problems. _____

7 Talia thinks that the English teacher is a good person to ask for help. _____

8 Talia says that Rakeem needs to stay at home tonight. _____

2 ▶ 9.3 Order the words to make sentences from the conversation. Then listen again and check.

1 you / work / take / off / some / time / can / from

_____?

2 should / not / I'm / sure / I

_____.

3 don't / talk / with / why / you / your / family

_____?

4 good / that's / a / idea

_____.

5 visiting / tomorrow / about / your / how / teacher / English

_____?

6 do / let's / fun / tonight / something

_____!

3 ▶ 9.4 Talia talks to Rakeem about a problem that she's having. Complete the conversation. Then listen and check.

Rakeem	Is everything okay with you, Talia?
Talia	Yes, but my roommate is very noisy. It's difficult to study there.
Rakeem	Oh no! I'm sorry to hear that. ¹_____ you look for another apartment?
Talia	I'm not sure I ²_____. It's expensive to change apartments.
Rakeem	³_____ you talk to your roommate? Tell her that you need to study. I'm sure she'll try her best to be quieter.
Talia	That's a ⁴_____ idea.
Rakeem	How ⁵_____ studying when she's not at home?
Talia	Yes, maybe. She's not there this weekend! ⁶_____ have dinner at my apartment tomorrow night.
Rakeem	That's a ⁷_____ idea!

4 Complete the phrases for sounding sympathetic.

1 You _____thing!

2 Oh no! I'm _____ to hear that!

3 That's a _____!

4 How _____!

5 ▶ 9.5 Listen to four situations. Respond using an expression from exercise 4. Sound sympathetic.

6 ▶ 9.6 Now listen to the situations again and write the response that you hear. Then listen again and repeat.

1 A I've fallen out with my sister. We're not speaking!

B _____.

2 A I'm having a lot of problems with my boyfriend.

B _____.

3 A That math exam was awful. I'm sure I failed it.

B _____.

4 A I lost my wallet! And it had all my money in it.

B _____.

HOME   BLOG   PODCASTS   ABOUT   CONTACT

Learning Curve

Tom and Sam talk about Belinda's school days.

LISTENING

1 ▶ 9.7 Listen to the podcast about Belinda's school days. Check (✔) the subjects you hear.

a PE   ____
b music   ____
c math   ____
d history   ____
e IT   ____
f languages   ____
g literature   ____
h art   ____
i geography   ____

2 ▶ 9.7 Listen again. Choose the correct options to answer the questions.

1 What kind of school did Belinda go to?
   a a school with no adults.
   b a school with no teachers.
2 Did Belinda like the school?
   a Yes, she was happy there.
   b No, she didn't like it.

3 ▶ 9.7 Listen again. Complete the sentences with one or two words.

1 Sam's favorite subjects were music _____.
2 Belinda finished school _____.
3 Now, she's studying art and _____ in college.
4 The adults at the school helped the students with any _____.
5 At the start of the week, the students worked in _____.
6 Belinda often went on trips to the _____ and _____.

READING

1 Read the blog on page 55 about someone who made a big change in his life. Number sentences a–e in the order the things happened (1–5).

a Aapo met lots of new people.   ____
b Aapo's friends gave him advice about how to be happier.   ____
c Aapo found out about an ice climbing club. ____
d Aapo decided not to go to college.   ____
e Aapo felt very unhappy with his life.

2 Use the information in the blog to answer the questions with one or two words.

1 How old was Aapo when he decided to make a change in his life?
   _____
2 Where did his friends tell him to go to get exercise?
   _____
3 What did Aapo see that sounded interesting?
   _____
4 What did Aapo decide to learn more about?
   _____
5 Which other activity is like ice climbing?
   _____
6 Where does Aapo live?
   _____
7 What do you have to do so that you don't fall when you're climbing?
   _____
8 What is different about Aapo's life now?
   _____

HOME   BLOG   PODCASTS   ABOUT   CONTACT

Guest blogger Taylor hears from a young man about how he changed his life.

LIFE CHANGES

Do you feel you need to make some resolutions? Perhaps you want to change your life, but you're not sure how to go about it? Here's Aapo Virtanen's story. He wanted to get in shape and lose weight, and thanks to a new hobby, everything changed.

It was a few months before my nineteenth birthday. I lived at home, didn't have a girlfriend, and I was overweight. School wasn't good either – I failed all my exams, and I didn't have the grades I needed to get into college. Nothing was going right!

My friends told me I needed to change. They said, "You should get more exercise and get in shape. And you really need to lose weight! Why not go to the gym?" But I don't like going to the gym – I just find it really boring. I wanted to do something different, but I wasn't sure what. Then I saw a poster about an ice climbing club. I didn't know what ice climbing was, but it sounded interesting, so I decided to find out more. I called the contact person and went to the first meeting. That was the beginning of a new life for me.

Ice climbing is an extreme sport. It's similar to rock climbing, but the rocks you climb are icy! I live in the north of Finland, so in the winter there is a lot of ice to climb. It's pretty dangerous, of course, but I love it. When you are ice climbing, you can't think about anything else. If you don't think carefully about what you are doing, you could fall. It makes your brain feel really alive, too. And I've made some great new friends doing it.

A year later, everything has changed – and everything's better! I'm in better shape, and I'm also very slim. I now realize that college isn't for me. I want to get a job so that I can earn money. I need to save a few hundred euros so that I can train to be an ice climbing teacher. Then I can ice climb all day, every day!

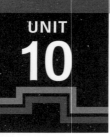

GRAMMAR: Comparative adjectives

1 Complete the sentences with the comparative form of the adjectives in parentheses.

1 My grandparents' house is _____ than ours. (big)

2 Sam was _____ than his older brother. (friendly)

3 This exercise is _____ than the last one. (easy)

4 Which is _____ – New York or Paris? (far)

5 These boots are _____ than your old ones. (nice)

6 Is the weather _____ in the spring or the fall? (bad)

7 Walking in town is _____ than bike riding. (safe)

8 The food in this café is _____ than my cooking! (good)

9 It was _____ yesterday than it is today. (hot)

10 The bus was _____ than the train. (fast)

2 Use the prompts to write sentences.

1 most stores / bit / expensive / the market

_____.

2 New York / much / crowded / my city

_____.

3 the library / quiet / our classroom

_____.

4 skiing / lot / dangerous / walking

_____!

5 the park / noisy / a club

_____.

6 your niece / smart / your nephew

_____?

VOCABULARY: Adjectives to describe places

3 Choose the correct options to complete the sentences.

1 We need to go shopping. The fridge and cabinets are _____!
   a safe **b** crowded **c** empty

2 I can't see anything at all outside. It's really _____.
   a ugly **b** dark **c** light

3 It can be _____ with so many fast cars on the road.
   a unfriendly **b** great **c** dangerous

4 Sasha didn't like her new school. Everyone was very _____.
   a beautiful **b** unfriendly **c** crowded

5 I made some vegetable soup yesterday, but it tasted _____!
   a horrible **b** ugly **c** dark

6 It was a _____ day, so they decided to go to the beach.
   a friendly **b** beautiful **c** safe

4 Complete the sentences with adjectives with the opposite meaning.

1 Everyone loves Anna. She's a really *unfriendly* _____ girl.

2 Is it *dangerous* _____ to go out at night in your city?

3 Look at that building! Don't you think it's *beautiful* _____?

4 The streets in this town aren't very *dark* _____ at night.

5 I don't like taking the bus because it's always *empty* _____.

6 This pizza is really *terrible* _____. Would you like some?

PRONUNCIATION: -er endings

5 ▶ 10.1 Say the sentences. How do we say the comparative adjectives? Listen, check, and repeat.

1 Her shoes were cheaper than mine.

2 The country is quieter than the city.

3 You're always busier than me!

4 Is your car safer than Alex's?

5 Anna was friendlier than her cousin.

6 Is Madrid bigger than Barcelona?

7 His hair was darker than yours.

8 It's noisier here than in class.

LISTENING: Listening for detailed information (1)

1 ▶10.2 You will hear an interview about a model agency. Check (✔) the words you think you'll hear. Then listen and check.

a	elderly	_____	e	bald	_____
b	slim	_____	f	young	_____
c	tall	_____	g	overweight	_____
d	thin	_____	h	middle-aged	_____

2 ▶10.2 Listen again. Write the words you hear instead of the underlined words.

1 He <u>owns</u> a model agency. _____
2 Their appearance is <u>very</u> different. _____
3 Many of us are <u>bored with</u> seeing beautiful models. _____
4 I <u>really liked</u> clothes and fashion. _____
5 Models don't always need to be <u>pretty</u>. _____
6 At first, it <u>wasn't easy</u>. _____

3 ▶10.2 Read the questions carefully. Then listen again and choose the correct answers.

1 When did Leon start his model agency business?
 a last year
 b five months ago
 c three years ago
2 What does Leon say about his models?
 a They don't look like most models.
 b They are all very beautiful.
 c They are all young.
3 Why didn't Leon become a model?
 a He didn't want to change his appearance.
 b He didn't like his hair.
 c He wanted a more traditional job.

4 What does Leon say is important for a model?
 a lots of clothes
 b a good appearance
 c his or her character
5 How successful is Leon's business?
 a It's not very successful at all.
 b It's doing better now.
 c It's changing all the time.

4 Order the letters to make appearance words.

1 D L N O B _____
2 U C Y L R _____
3 G R R E I N A _____
4 S T H C M U E A _____
5 A F I R _____
6 M M D U I E - H E L N T G _____
7 Y G R A _____
8 A B E D R D E _____
9 N P G I I R C E _____
10 S S S G L A E _____

5 ▶10.3 Read the sentences and underline the words that you think have weak forms. Listen and check.

1 I mean, their appearance is pretty different!
2 My models are very different from usual models.
3 What an interesting idea!
4 At first, it was difficult.
5 People like looking at my models.

GRAMMAR: Superlative adjectives

1 Complete the sentences with the superlative forms of the adjectives in the box.

> good   bad   big   safe
> crowded   old   far   friendly

1 This magazine says that _____ person in the country is 112!
2 Which is _____ star from Earth?
3 Alberto won a competition for _____ painting in the art class.
4 That's _____ cake in the store! We only need a small one.
5 What's _____ city in Europe? I want to go traveling on my own.
6 I got _____ score on the test – I didn't get any answers right!
7 Mumbai is _____ city in India. About twenty million people live there.
8 Who is _____ teacher in your school?

2 Complete the text with the correct words.

I go to a photography club every Thursday, and last week we gave out end-of-year prizes. Everybody likes Sara, so we decided she was the ¹_____ popular girl in the club. Ben is friends with everyone – so he got a prize for ²_____ nicest person. Lucy always takes fantastic pictures – she got a prize for the ³_____ photo. But Mara took the ⁴_____ exciting photo – it was of a car race. Her dad had the ⁵_____ car, so he won. It was a great evening, and I was really happy. In fact, I think it was one of the ⁶_____ days of my life!

VOCABULARY: Personality adjectives

3 Order the letters to make personality adjectives.

1 He is very *neitcdonf* in France because he speaks French well.
_____
2 She's really *onersgue*. She always gets me a birthday present.
_____
3 It is important to be *tolepi* by opening doors for people.
_____
4 I like *relfhuec* people who smile a lot.
_____
5 She is not very *kavtlieta*. I think she is shy.
_____
6 My sister is really *sratm*. She passed all her exams.
_____

4 Complete the personality adjectives.

1 Max can't swim, so he was very b_____ to jump into the water.
2 We all laugh a lot when Wahid's here. He's a really f_____ student.
3 "Can I carry your bag for you?" "Thanks, that's extremely k_____."
4 Our cat's very l_____. It sleeps most of the day.
5 My sister's not s_____ at all – she makes friends with everyone.
6 Everyone likes my chemistry teacher, but my music teacher's not very p_____.

PRONUNCIATION: Superlative adjectives

5 ▶10.4 Say the sentences. How do we say the superlative adjectives? Listen, check, and repeat.

1 What's the most exciting place in the world?
2 She's the kindest girl I know.
3 He is the laziest boy in the school.
4 Ella is the most popular girl in the club.
5 It's the funniest movie of the year.
6 Who's the most relaxed person in your family?
7 Is she the most beautiful woman in the country?
8 My nicest present was this necklace.

WRITING: Writing a description of a person

A WOMAN I ADMIRE

A Florence Nightingale was born in 1820 in Florence, Italy, but her family was British. After a year, they moved back to England. Later, Florence became a nurse and helped a lot of people. She was an attractive, slim woman with long brown hair and a lovely smile.

B Florence's parents wanted her to get married, but she decided to travel and to learn about the science of nursing. She was a nurse in hospitals in Turkey during the Crimean war against Russia. These hospitals were dangerous and very dirty, and it was extremely difficult working there. Florence tried very hard to make the hospitals cleaner and safer places.

C I admire Florence Nightingale because she was strong and one of the bravest women at that time. Women usually stayed at home then, but Florence did what she thought was right. Her story inspired me, and I want to be a nurse, too.

1 Read the text about Florence Nightingale. Which paragraphs give the information below? Write A, B, or C.

1 why the writer admires her _____
2 facts about her life _____
3 where she was from _____
4 what she believed _____
5 what her job was _____
6 what she looked like _____

2 Complete the sentences about Florence Nightingale. Use a verb from the box in the simple past.

| travel | make | do | work | not be |
| be (x2) | not want | help | want | become |

1 Florence Nightingale _____ Italian, but she _____ born in Italy.
2 She _____ to get married. She _____ a nurse, instead.
3 She _____ to learn about nursing, so she _____ to Turkey.
4 She _____ in hospitals in Turkey and tried to make them safer.
5 She _____ a lot of soldiers and _____ what she thought was right.
6 She _____ a brave and attractive woman, and _____ a real difference to people's lives.

3 Join the sentences using a clause with *when*. Write two versions for each sentence.

Example

When she was young, she lived in Italy. / She lived in Italy when she was young.

1 Florence was a baby. That's when her family moved to England.

_____

_____

2 There was a war against Russia. At that time, Florence worked as a nurse.

_____

_____

3 Florence was young. At that time, women usually stayed at home.

_____

_____

4 Write a description of someone you admire. Include the information below:

Paragraph 1: Where is he/she from? What does he/she do? What does he/she look like?

Paragraph 2: What are the important events and achievements in his/her life?

Paragraph 3: Why do you admire this person?

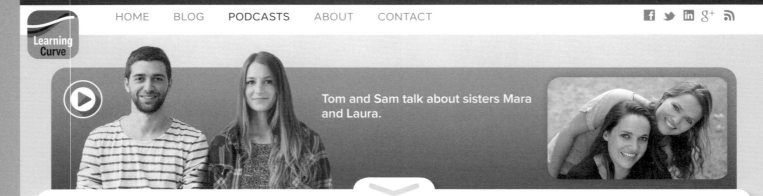

HOME   BLOG   **PODCASTS**   ABOUT   CONTACT

Tom and Sam talk about sisters Mara and Laura.

LISTENING

1 ▶ **10.5** Listen to the podcast about two sisters. Choose the correct answers.

  1 What do Mara and Laura do?
    a Mara's a theater director and Laura's an actress.
    b They're both actresses.

  2 Do they have similar personalities and appearance?
    a Yes, they do.
    b No, they don't.

2 ▶ **10.5** Listen again. Are the sentences about Mara (M) or Laura (L)?

  1 She was a quiet and polite child. ____
  2 She's two years older than her sister. ____
  3 She's tall and slim. ____
  4 She has long, black hair. ____
  5 She's a little overweight. ____
  6 She has brown, curly hair. ____

3 ▶ **10.5** Listen again. Are the sentences true (T) or false (F)?

  1 Mara works at a theater in Madrid. ____
  2 Laura is less famous than her sister. ____
  3 Mara often has a lot of problems with Laura. ____
  4 Mara often plays talkative or funny characters. ____
  5 Mara prefers the parts that her sister plays. ____

READING

1 Read the blog on page 61 about some of the best places in the world to visit. What does the blog say? Choose the correct options to complete the sentences.

  1 The best view is from the *Grand Canyon* / *Mount Ararat*.
  2 Reykjavik is one of the *coldest* / *friendliest* cities.
  3 The people in Auckland are very *kind* / *shy*.
  4 Switzerland is the *most dangerous* / *safest* country.
  5 Scottish people are the *nicest* / *most talkative*.

2 Complete the sentences with one or two words from the blog.

  1 Mount Ararat is a very tall _____ in Turkey.
  2 Readers decided that the _____ city in the world is Auckland.
  3 One reader said that he/she talked to lots of _____ when he/she was in New Zealand.
  4 The places that are safe to visit aren't always _____, as well.
  5 A female traveler said she was happy walking in _____ of Switzerland at night.
  6 Readers said that the Czech Republic, Denmark, and Canada were also very _____ places.
  7 The _____ food was the deep-fried bar of chocolate.

HOME   **BLOG**   PODCASTS   ABOUT   CONTACT

Tom and Sam look at the best and worst places to visit.

▷ # You have your say

We all love traveling, but what are the best – and the worst – places to go to? Here are some of our readers' ideas. Do you agree with them?

BEST VIEW

Many people think that the best view is the Grand Canyon in Arizona, but 60% of our readers say that Mount Ararat in Turkey is even more beautiful! This 5,000-meter-high volcano is an awesome sight – if you go there, take a picnic and make sure you have your camera with you!

FRIENDLIEST CITY

We often think of cities as crowded places where people never stop to speak to each other. It doesn't have to be this way! Many of you voted for Reykjavik in Iceland. The weather may be cold, but the people are not unfriendly – lots of our readers wrote in to say how kind and welcoming people in this city are. However, in our readers' opinion, the people of Auckland, New Zealand are even happier to talk. One traveler said, "I can't count the number of times strangers came up and started speaking to me. And on a three-week visit I got invited to dinner five times. Wow!"

SAFEST COUNTRY FOR VISITORS

Sadly, some of the most exciting countries in the world can also be quite dangerous. But safe doesn't have to mean boring. Our readers voted the lovely mountainous Switzerland as the safest country to visit. One female traveler said, "I feel totally safe walking around at night, even when it's dark, and the streets are empty." Sounds good to us! Denmark, Canada, and the Czech Republic were also on the top of the safe places list.

WORST DISH

We're sorry, Scotland, but the prize goes to you! Many people voted for a deep-fried chocolate bar. One reader said, "This was horrible. I need to lose weight! I didn't want to eat a deep-fried dessert." We hope our Scottish readers don't feel too bad though – our readers also think Scotland has the nicest people!

UNIT 11 On the move

11A — LANGUAGE

GRAMMAR: *Have to/don't have to*

1 Choose the correct options to complete the sentences.

1 She _____ save money because she's going to college next year.

   a have to   **b** don't have to   **c** has to

2 Do you _____ take the train or can you ride your bike?

   a have to   **b** have   **c** has to

3 He _____ go to work this morning.

   a have to   **b** doesn't have to
   c don't have to

4 You _____ wash the dishes – I can do it.

   a don't have to   **b** have to   **c** has to

5 We _____ visit our grandfather tomorrow.

   a has to   **b** doesn't have to   **c** have to

6 I _____ have to go to bed early because it's Saturday!

   a has   **b** don't   **c** doesn't

7 She _____ do her homework before she can play online games.

   a has to   **b** have to   **c** don't have to

8 Are you coming to New Zealand? You _____ visit me!

   a doesn't have to   **b** has to   **c** have to

2 Complete the e-mail with the correct form of *have to/don't have to*.

○○○

Dear Maria,

How are you? Dad and I are both well. Ella is working in a store on Saturdays because she ¹_____ to save money to buy clothes! What is your house like? Is it near your college? Do you ²_____ to take the bus, or can you walk? I hope you ³_____ have to get up too early in the morning! Are you eating well? Remember, it ⁴_____ have to be expensive to cook a delicious meal. I hope you can come home next weekend for your brother's birthday. So you don't ⁵_____ to do your wash this week, I can do it when you're here. What are you doing tomorrow? I ⁶_____ have to get up early because it's Sunday. And your father? Yes, he ⁷_____ because he ⁸_____ walk the dog!

Love from Mom X

VOCABULARY: Travel and transportation

3 Order the letters to make words for travel and transportation.

1 The New York *yuwsba* _____ is often very crowded.

2 When my grandmother was 80, she had a ride in a *poctrelieh* _____.

3 You have to wear a helmet to travel by *toromylcec* _____.

4 Lots of people travel by *restoco* _____ in Italy.

5 Our *rryef* _____ takes five hours to cross the sea.

6 I prefer to travel by *sbu* _____. It's cheap and relaxing.

4 Look at the pictures. Write the words.

1 _____   3 _____   5 _____

2 _____   4 _____   6 _____

PRONUNCIATION: *have to/has to*

5 ▶ 11.1 Say the sentences. How do we say *have to* and *has to*? Listen, check, and repeat.

1 Does she have to speak English at work?

2 Do you have to go to bed early?

3 He doesn't have to cook this evening.

4 He has to finish his homework.

5 You have to visit me in Turkey.

6 I don't have to work tomorrow.

READING: Reading for detail

Two friends, two different opinions ...

Best friends Cara and Vanessa went on vacation together for the first time this summer. Are they still friends? Read and find out!

Vanessa

I was so happy when Cara and I decided to go on vacation together this summer. Cara is my best friend, and I was really looking forward to it. In the end, though, it wasn't so great.

Cara is very energetic, but I like to relax on vacation. She wanted to take the train and go sightseeing in different towns and cities – but I wanted to stay on the beach! She said, "You're on vacation! You have to see things! You can't just sleep all the time."

We spent a lot of money on sightseeing and other activities. I don't think you have to spend money to have fun. Maybe Cara disagrees with that, though!

We will definitely stay friends, but we probably won't go on vacation together again.

Cara

Vanessa is a really great friend, and we had a wonderful vacation together. She was a bit tired sometimes – maybe that was just because the weather was too hot.

We did so many fun things – we took a ferry to a little island, we walked for miles through beautiful countryside, and I think we saw all the sights, too. One day we even did a parachute jump! That was certainly my favorite part of the trip.

Next summer, we're probably going on vacation together again. Possibly a sports vacation next time? I can't wait!

1 Look at the title and the pictures. What do you think the text is about?

  a two friends who had a great vacation together

  b two friends who don't feel the same about their vacation

  c two friends who had a terrible vacation together

2 Read the questions and options. Fill in the blanks with the words in the box. There are two extra words.

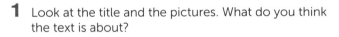

do Cara best time Vanessa feel money

1 How did Vanessa _____ before she went on vacation with Cara?

  a happy and excited

  b tired and sad

  c bored

2 What did Vanessa want to _____ on vacation?

  a go sightseeing

  b relax on the beach

  c travel by train

3 Why did they spend a lot of _____?

  a Their hotel was expensive.

  b They ate in expensive restaurants.

  c They did a lot of sightseeing.

4 What did Cara like _____ about the trip?

  a the parachute jump

  b the weather

  c the ferry trip

5 What type of vacation does _____ want them to go on next year?

  a a beach vacation

  b a sports vacation

  c a shopping vacation

3 Now choose the correct options to answer the questions in exercise 2.

4 Order the words to make sentences.

1 go on vacation / I / with Vanessa / want to / next year /definitely

_____

2 prefers / vacations / maybe / relaxing / Vanessa

_____

3 spent / we / too / money / much / probably

_____

4 going on / sports vacation / a / next summer / possibly / we're

_____

5 enjoyed / her / my vacation / I / with / certainly

_____

6 our friend / is going / to come / next year / Mandy / perhaps

_____

GRAMMAR: *Be going to* and future time expressions

1 Choose the correct options to complete the sentences.

1 *Are / Is / Am* your girlfriend going to come with us?

2 I *'m not / 're not / 's not* going to finish all these French fries.

3 "Are you going to eat that slice of bread?" "Yes, I *is / are / am*."

4 They *'s not going / not going / 're not going* to stay at a hotel.

5 "Is he going to be late for class again?" "No, he *'s not / 're not / is*."

6 *Are / Is / Am* you going to buy some new clothes?

7 We *isn't going / are going / not going* to visit Paris this month.

8 "Are the children going to get dressed soon?" "Yes, they *aren't / is / are*."

2 Complete the text with the correct form of *going to*.

I'm really excited about my plans for the summer. First, I ¹_____ work for two weeks in a café. I ²_____ go out because I have to save money. After that, my cousin Kinga ³_____ come to visit me from Hungary. We ⁴_____ go traveling around Europe. I can't wait! Her parents ⁵_____ come to my house, too, but they ⁶ _____ go traveling with us. Kinga and I ⁷_____ take the bus – the train is much faster. Where ⁸_____ stay? I don't know yet! But I know it ⁹ _____ be anywhere expensive, because Kinga ¹⁰_____ have much money.

VOCABULARY: Vacation activities

3 Choose the correct options to complete the e-mail.

Hi Carla,

I'm having a great time here in Crete! It's a really beautiful place. We're ¹____ at a hotel near the sea. You know I love relaxing on the ²____ or ³____ the pool, so this is perfect for me! We're here for ten days before we come home.

There's only one problem. Mom and Dad want us to ⁴____ sightseeing and visit ⁵____. I don't want to! It's really hot, and I don't enjoy looking at old buildings!

My brother Sam is having a lot of fun, too. He ⁶____ surfing all day, every day!

See you soon,
Daphne

1	**a** staying	**b** going	**c** visiting
2	**a** mountains	**b** beach	**c** surfing
3	**a** by	**b** on	**c** to
4	**a** be	**b** get	**c** go
5	**a** campsites	**b** museums	**c** mountains
6	**a** has	**b** does	**c** goes

4 Complete the sentences.

1 We went on v_____ to Florida. It rained every day!

2 I really want to go swimming. Can we go to the b_____ later?

3 In the summer, I love sitting by the p_____ reading a book.

4 We enjoy walking, so we're going h_____ in Peru.

5 Where did you stay? Were you at a c_____ ?

6 Mario loves old paintings – he wants to v_____ an art gallery tomorrow.

PRONUNCIATION: Sentence stress

5 ▶11.2 Say the sentences. Listen and repeat.

1 I'm going to stay with friends.

2 We're going to be more organized.

3 You're not going to run a marathon.

4 He's not going to have an interview.

5 Is she going to swim with us?

6 Are you going to see Ernesto tonight?

SPEAKING: Checking information

1 ⏵**11.3** Listen to the conversation at a hotel. Choose the correct answers.

1 Mr Gutiérrez is staying at the Amberton Hotel for ____ nights.
   a three   **b** four   **c** five

2 He is staying on the ____ floor.
   a seventh   **b** eighth   **c** ninth

3 They start breakfast at ____ in the morning.
   a seven   **b** eight   **c** nine

2 ⏵**11.3** Complete the conversation with the words in the box. Listen again and check.

> spell   checking   password   sign   reservation
> floor   reserved   key   breakfast   ID

Receptionist	Good afternoon. Welcome to the Amberton Hotel. ¹_____ in?
Mr Gutiérrez	Yes. I have a ²_____ under the name of Gutiérrez.
Receptionist	Could you ³_____ your last name, please?
Mr Gutiérrez	Yes, it's G-U-T-I-E-R-R-E-Z.
Receptionist	You've ⁴_____ for three nights and are checking out on Friday. Is that correct?
Mr Gutiérrez	Yes, that's right.
Receptionist	Ah, yes. Can I have your ⁵_____, please?
Mr Gutiérrez	Yes, of course.
Receptionist	Can you ⁶_____ this form, please? OK. Here's your ⁷_____. You're on the ninth floor.
Mr Gutiérrez	What's the WiFi ⁸_____?
Receptionist	It's Amberton, the name of the hotel.
Mr Gutiérrez	Great, thanks! And what time is ⁹_____?
Receptionist	It's from seven to nine.
Mr Gutiérrez	Thank you. Which ¹⁰_____ did you say? The eighth?
Receptionist	The ninth. Enjoy your stay.
Mr Gutiérrez	Thank you!

3 Complete the phrases to check information.

1 You've reserved for six nights and are checking out on Friday. Is that _____?

2 Thank you. My room's on the seventh floor, _____?

3 _____ you say breakfast starts at eight thirty?

4 Are the phrases in exercise 3 formal (F), neutral (N), or informal (I)?

1 ____
2 ____
3 ____

5 ⏵**11.4** Listen to five sentences. Who says them? Write receptionist (R) or guest (G).

1 ____
2 ____
3 ____
4 ____
5 ____

6 ⏵**11.4** Listen again. Respond and check the information with the receptionist or guest.

7 You are a guest in a hotel. Respond to the receptionist's comments. Use a formal (F), neutral (N), or informal (I) phrase.

1 **Receptionist** "Dinner is from 7:30 p.m. to 9:45 p.m."
   You _____ (N).

2 **Receptionist** "The price for a double room is $125."
   You _____ (F).

3 **Receptionist** "There's WiFi in every room."
   You _____ (I).

4 **Receptionist** "Your room is on the eleventh floor."
   You _____ (N).

5 **Receptionist** "There's a gym in the hotel."
   You _____ (F).

6 **Receptionist** "Breakfast's not included in the price."
   You _____ (N).

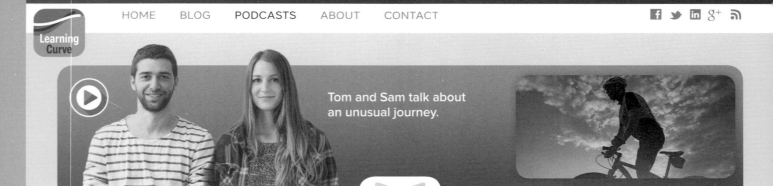

HOME   BLOG   PODCASTS   ABOUT   CONTACT

Tom and Sam talk about an unusual journey.

LISTENING

1 ▶ **11.5** Listen to the podcast about an unusual trip. Are the sentences about Ben true (T) or false (F)?

1 He finished his trip in the spring.   ____
2 He is traveling to places that begin with the same letter.   ____
3 He is planning to visit the beach.   ____
4 He will go sightseeing in Bolivia.   ____
5 He is going to Tokyo next year.   ____

2 ▶ **11.5** Listen again. Choose the correct answers.

1 Where did Ben start his trip after his flight?
   a Belgium
   b Britain
   c Budapest

2 How is Ben going to travel to Bolivia?
   a by plane
   b by bike
   c by bus

3 Ben's not working for ____ months.
   a three
   b four
   c six

4 What does Ben say is interesting about Bosnia?
   a its beaches
   b the history
   c everything

5 Where will Ben go surfing?
   a Bosnia
   b Belize
   c Bolivia

6 Which of the places <u>doesn't</u> Ben mention?
   a Toledo
   b Tokyo
   c Turkey

READING

1 Read the blog on page 67 about vacation jobs. Complete the sentences with *Kyra*, *Oliver*, or *Stefano*.

1 _____ had a job working with older people.
2 _____ is going to teach children art.
3 _____ stayed at a campsite last year.
4 _____ went to the Mediterranean.
5 _____ worked in two different countries.
6 _____ likes working with children.

2 Are the sentences true (T), false (F), or doesn't say (DS)?

1 You need a lot of money to travel around the world.   ____
2 You have to be in shape to pick fruit.   ____
3 Picking fruit is an easy job and it pays well.   ____
4 Kyra ate a lot of fruit when she was in France.   ____
5 You can do different kinds of jobs on a cruise ship.   ____
6 Oliver didn't like working on a cruise ship   ____
7 The people working on a cruise ship have to be young.   ____
8 You have to like children to work at some campsites.   ____
9 Stefano is going to teach the children English.   ____
10 At the vacation camp, the children can go hiking.   ____

HOME   BLOG   PODCASTS   ABOUT   CONTACT

Guest blogger Penny writes about working in different countries.

Work your way around the world

Do you want to go traveling, but you have no money? Don't worry! You don't have to be rich to see the world. There are lots of ways you can visit different countries and earn money at the same time. Here are some of my top ideas.

FRESH AIR AND FRUIT

This is a popular way for young people to travel the world. You can pick grapes in France, oranges in Spain, and olives in Greece. You have to be in shape and enjoy outdoor life, but it's a lot of fun, and you can make friends from lots of different countries. Kyra Scott traveled around Europe picking fruit last year: "I started in the UK, where I picked strawberries. Then I went to France and picked peaches. It can be hard work, and I didn't earn much money. But I made enough to pay for the campsite and to buy food. I also had as much fruit as I could eat – I don't think I ever want to see another strawberry!"

SAIL AWAY

Cruise ships take thousands of vacationers every year to some of the world's most beautiful towns and cities, so they're always looking for staff to wash dishes, serve food, or clean the cabins. You have to work long hours, but the pay can be pretty good. Oliver Baum worked on a cruise ship this summer, traveling around the Mediterranean: "It was a fantastic experience. The guests were all elderly, and they were mostly really polite and friendly. I really enjoyed looking after them!"

WORK AT A VACATION CAMP

If you like working with other people, why not look for a job at a campsite? Vacation camps are always looking for young people to help with entertainment and activities. If you like children, this can be an excellent job. Stefano Rossi says: "I'm going to work at a campsite in Spain next year. I'm going to look after children in the morning. They do painting and drama and lots of other activities, like surfing. You don't have to speak Spanish, as lots of the vacationers are American or British – but it helps if you do!"

You see? No money – no problem! Start making your travel plans now!

Enjoy yourself

12A — LANGUAGE

GRAMMAR: Present perfect with *ever* and *never*

1 Order the words to make sentences and questions in the present perfect.

1 ever / you / the Northern Lights / seen / have

_____?

2 have / a blog / written / they / never

_____.

3 has / this book / read / he / ever

_____?

4 gone / never / together / we've / bowling

_____

5 ever / we / your sister-in-law / have / met

_____?

6 has / never / karate / done / he

_____

2 Complete the conversation with the present perfect form of the verbs in parentheses.

Marta	I'm having a party on Saturday! Do you want to help? I need to be really organized!
Piotr	¹_____ (I/never/organize) a party before. But I'd love to help!
Marta	Great, thanks.
	²_____ (you/ever/make) pizza?
Piotr	No, ³_____ (I/not)!
Marta	That's OK. ⁴_____ (I/never/make) one either!
Piotr	⁵_____ (Sam/ever/cook) for a party? We could ask him.
Marta	Great idea! ⁶_____ (he/have) lots of parties. ⁷_____ (I/be) to some of them.
Piotr	But ⁸_____ (I/not/see) him this week. Is he at home?
Marta	Oh no! I remember now. ⁹_____ (he/leave) to visit his aunt and uncle in Germany! He comes back next week.

VOCABULARY: Entertainment

3 Complete the text with the words in the box. There is one extra word.

concerts   artist   singer   match   exhibit   bands   opera

Although my town is small, there's a lot to do. This weekend, I went to a really interesting art ¹_____ at the gallery near my house. I saw some beautiful paintings. I met the ²_____ and it was really interesting hearing him talk about his work. My city is also famous for music. There's a festival every year, and many ³_____ from different countries come to play. There's a small jazz club near my house, too. It stays open late and has great ⁴_____! If you prefer classical music, you can see an ⁵_____. I love the music – when I was younger I wanted to be an opera ⁶_____. It didn't happen, but I still love watching and dreaming!

4 Complete the words.

1 We love movies with Daniel Radcliffe. He's a brilliant a_____r.

2 The basketball p_____s were really happy when their team won.

3 I saw *Swan Lake* at the theater last night. It's my favorite b_____t.

4 How many m_____s are in the band?

5 I don't mind watching baseball on TV, but I've never been to a g_____e.

6 There were two d_____s and a traditional Spanish guitarist in the show.

PRONUNCIATION: Sentence stress

5 ▶12.1 Say the sentences. Listen and repeat.

1 Have you ever been to this gallery?

2 I've never played the violin.

3 I've served food in a café.

4 Have you ever been to a rock concert?

5 I haven't tried Vietnamese food.

6 I haven't been to Canada.

7 I've been to Poland.

8 I've never written a song.

LISTENING: Listening for detailed information (2)

1 ▶12.2 Listen to the conversation about birthdays. Which adjectives describe the things below?

1 Layla's last birthday	*amazing / boring / terrible*
2 Peter's last birthday	*stupid / awesome / strange*
3 the ending of the movie	*sad / interesting / exciting*
4 the Thanksgiving costumes	*awful / scary / fun*

2 ▶12.2 Listen again. Choose the correct answers.

1 Who is Ben?
  a Layla's father
  b Layla's friend
  c Layla's cousin

2 How did Layla get to Vancouver?
  a by bus
  b by train
  c by car

3 Who took Peter to see a play?
  a his girlfriend
  b Layla
  c his best friend

4 When is Layla's birthday?
  a November 22nd
  b November 23rd
  c November 24th

5 What kind of party does Peter suggest?
  a a surprise party
  b a costume party
  c a strange party

3 Listen again. Answer the questions. Write complete sentences.

1 How many of Layla's friends and family were on the train to Vancouver?

_____

2 How long did Layla and her friends and family go to Vancouver for?

_____

3 How did Peter's girlfriend feel after the movie?

_____

4 Has Layla had a costume party before?

_____

4 ▶12.3 Read the sentences. Mark the links between words. Listen, check, and repeat.

1 Last year I had an amazing birthday.
2 My cousin organized a surprise party for me.
3 I thought I was going to see an action movie.
4 Everyone can get dressed up in really fun costumes.
5 I had one when I was eight years old.

GRAMMAR: Present perfect and simple past

1 Choose the correct options to complete the sentences.

1 We _____ Cara last night. She looked great.
   a have seen
   b saw

2 _____ a letter to a famous person as a child?
   a Have you ever written
   b Did you ever write

3 Last week they _____ the new pizza restaurant.
   a tried
   b have tried

4 I _____ any of the *Harry Potter* movies.
   a have never seen
   b never saw

5 When _____ to the gym this morning?
   a have you been
   b did you go

6 She _____ her boyfriend in school.
   a met
   b has met

7 Where _____ that new watch?
   a have you bought
   b did you buy

8 "Has she ever been to Mexico?" "No, she _____ ."
   a didn't
   b hasn't

9 How _____ on their exams last month?
   a did they do
   b have they done

10 "Have your grandparents ever used a smartphone?" "No, they _____ ."
   a haven't
   b didn't

11 Who _____ at the party yesterday?
   a have you spoken to
   b did you speak to

12 They _____ to Brazil before.
   a have never been
   b haven't never gone

2 Complete the conversations. Use the simple past or present perfect form of the verbs in the box.

| not buy | drive | not eat | fly | go (x2) |
| have | meet | not read | not see | speak |

1 _____ you ever _____ in a helicopter?

2 I _____ you yesterday. I missed you!

3 I _____ any Russian novels. They're all so long!

4 Matt _____ never _____ sushi. He hates fish!

5 _____ she ever _____ a dog?

6 Jan and Mo _____ shopping last weekend, but they _____ anything.

7 _____ you _____ to the meeting, or _____ you _____ by train?

8 I _____ never _____ to Sue. What's she like?

3 Complete the conversation with the present perfect or simple past form of the verbs in parentheses.

Julia   ¹_____ camping, Matteo? (you/ever/go)

Matteo   Yes, I ²_____ last summer. (go)

Julia   And ³_____ you _____ it? (enjoy)

Matteo   It was awesome! ⁴_____ a fantastic time. (we/have)

Julia   Who ⁵_____ with? (you/go)

Matteo   I went with Sara and her family. ⁶_____ Sara? (you/meet)

Julia   No, I ⁷_____ (have). How long ⁸_____ for? (you/go)

Matteo   Five days. How about you? What ⁹_____ last summer? (you/do)

Julia   I ¹⁰_____ around the U.S. with my cousin. (travel) It was amazing!

PRONUNCIATION: Vowels

4 ▶12.4 Match the past participles that have the same vowel sound. Listen, check, and repeat.

1 worn   _____   a won
2 written _____   b spoken
3 drunk   _____   c eaten
4 seen   _____   d driven
5 flown   _____   e met
6 read   _____   f bought

WRITING: Writing and replying to an invitation

Jan and Bob
are 1_____
A HOUSEWARMING PARTY!

We'd love to welcome you to our new home.

Where: 12 Pine Street

When: Saturday, August 20th at 8 p.m.

Children are welcome.

Hope you 2_____ make it!

3_____: bob25@starmail.com

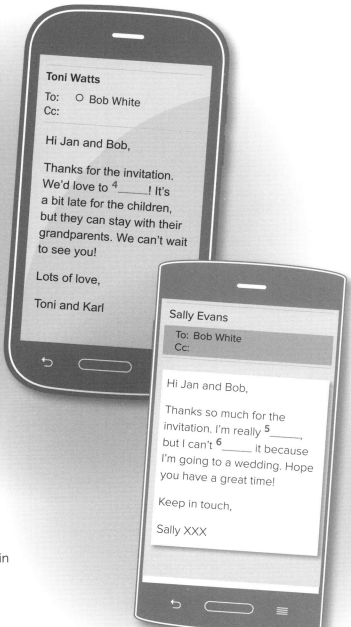

Toni Watts

To: ○ Bob White
Cc:

Hi Jan and Bob,

Thanks for the invitation. We'd love to 4_____! It's a bit late for the children, but they can stay with their grandparents. We can't wait to see you!

Lots of love,

Toni and Karl

Sally Evans

To: Bob White
Cc:

Hi Jan and Bob,

Thanks so much for the invitation. I'm really 5_____, but I can't 6_____ it because I'm going to a wedding. Hope you have a great time!

Keep in touch,

Sally XXX

1 Complete the invitations and replies with the words in the box.

come   RSVP   sorry   make   having   can

2 Jan and Toni are talking on the phone. Complete their conversation with *a*, *an*, *the*, or – (no article).

Jan Hi Toni! Do you have 1_____ recipe for pizza?

Toni Sure! Is it for 2_____ housewarming party on Saturday?

Jan Yes – I love 3_____ pizza, but I don't have a recipe for it.

Toni I can make some and bring it to your house before 4_____ party.

Jan Really? That's so kind of you!

Toni No problem. It's 12 Pine Street, right?

Jan That's right! There's 5_____ bus stop right in front. Thanks, Toni!

3 Reply to Jan and Bob's invitation. Use key phrases from exercise 1 and follow this structure:

* say hello
* say thanks
* decline the invitation
* say why
* say goodbye

4 Write an invitation to a party. Remember to include:

* the type of party
* the date and time
* your address
* other important information

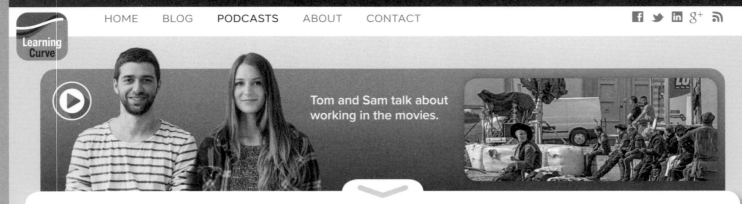

HOME   BLOG   **PODCASTS**   ABOUT   CONTACT

Tom and Sam talk about working in the movies.

LISTENING

1 ▶ 12.5 Listen to the podcast about a job working in the movies. Check (✔) the adjectives you hear.

a fantastic _____

b cool _____

c exciting _____

d fun _____

e great _____

f amazing _____

g boring _____

h interesting _____

2 ▶ 12.5 Listen again and choose the correct options to complete the sentences.

1 What are "extras" in a movie?

a They're the people in the background behind the actors. They don't speak.

b They're the people behind the cameras. They help the director.

2 Does Mikael like being an extra?

a Yes, he does. He loves it.

b He doesn't mind it, but he says it's sometimes boring.

3 ▶ 12.5 Listen again. Are the sentences true (T) or false (F)?

1 Extras do the same thing every day. _____

2 They usually start work early in the morning. _____

3 They have to wait a lot. _____

4 Mikael doesn't like waiting. _____

5 He's met some famous people. _____

6 He was a teacher in a *Harry Potter* movie. _____

7 He's also been an extra on TV. _____

8 He loves working in film studios. _____

9 He'd like to work in an office. _____

READING

1 Read the blog on page 73 about a singing group.

1 What kind of music does Ivor's group sing?

a music for young people

b opera music

c popular music

2 Who is the group for?

a happy people

b people the same age as Ivor

c people who have been to the opera a lot

2 Read the sentences. Are they true (T), false (F), or doesn't say (DS)?

1 Most teenagers like opera. _____

2 Ivor has sung in 50 different operas. _____

3 Reports show that singing makes people feel tired. _____

4 Lots of people want to join Ivor's opera group. _____

5 It is difficult to become a member of the group. _____

6 The group will only sing songs from popular operas. _____

7 The group doesn't make any money from singing. _____

8 Being in the group has helped some people's confidence. _____

3 Circle the opinion adjectives in the blog.

HOME   BLOG   PODCASTS   ABOUT   CONTACT

Tom and Sam look at making singing fun.

Singing for fun

What do you think when you hear the word "opera"? You might think "boring"! It's true that opera's not always popular with young people. Eighteen-year-old Ivor Golanski is trying to change that. In this special guest blog post, Ivor writes about his opera group "Singing for fun".

Many people my age have never been to the opera. I think that's sad and a little strange. I've been to about 50 operas in my life, and every time has been an awesome experience. So I decided that I wanted to start my own opera group for young people.

I've read reports that show how singing together can help people who are feeling tired or unhappy. When you sing, the body produces special chemicals that make you feel happy and relaxed. Singing together is fun, because when there are a lot of voices, it doesn't matter if you sing a wrong note – no one will hear it, so you won't feel stupid!

You don't have to be a great singer to join my group – but, of course, you can't have a terrible voice either! There are twenty members in the group now, and it's growing all the time. We always have a good time when we meet. Everyone works really hard, but we have a lot of fun together, as well.

We've already had a few concerts, where we sang songs from some well-known operas that lots of people know and like. We've sung in schools, at the city hall, and in our local theater. We haven't traveled to any other towns yet, but we'd like to. We're saving the money we make, and next year we'd like to go on a big tour.

Many people in the group tell me how singing has helped them in lots of ways. One member said, "Before I joined the opera group, I'd never been on stage. It was too scary! I'd only ever sung in the shower and thought I probably had a horrible voice. Now I feel much more confident about myself – my dream is to sing to a soccer stadium full of people!"

WRITING: Opening and closing an informal e-mail

● ○ ○

Hello Bella,

How are you? I hope everything's OK in Italy.

It's nice to meet you. My name's Andreas, and I'm eighteen years old. I'm from Germany, but I'm in the U.S. right now. I'm studying English at a language school. It's great here, but I don't like the weather – it's very hot!

I speak English every day with my host family. My host mother is a doctor, and she doesn't have a lot of free time. She has two sons: Andy and Greg. Greg is eighteen, and Andy is sixteen. They are both students.

On the weekend, we go shopping, or we play sports. Sometimes we go to the movies – there are some really good movie theaters here.

Write soon!

Andreas

1 Read Andreas's e-mail to a penpal. Complete the sentences.

1 Andreas is from _____.

2 He is eighteen _____ old.

3 Right now, Andreas is in _____.

4 He _____ the weather there.

5 He _____ sports on weekends.

2 Complete the sentences with *and*, *but*, or *or*.

1 Andreas is German, _____ he's eighteen.

Printed in Mexico by Impregráfica Digital, S.A. de C.V.
España 385, Col. San Nicolás Tolentino, C.P. 09850, Iztapalapa, Ciudad de México.

2 Andreas can speak German _____ English.

3 He's from Germany, _____ now he is in the U.S.

4 He likes the U.S., _____ the weather is too hot.

5 He plays sports _____ he goes shopping on the weekend.

3 Are the words and phrases for opening (O) or closing (C) an informal e-mail?

1 Hi   O   C

2 See you soon   O   C

3 Hey   O   C

4 Take care   O   C

5 Hello   O   C

6 Write soon   O   C

4 Write an e-mail to a new friend.

- introduce yourself
- say your name, age, and where you live
- use informal language to open and close your e-mail

WRITING: Describing a photo

Hi Malu,

How are you? How's your new job?

I know you like movies, so I'm sending you some photos of me with my movie club. We make movies together on Tuesday and Friday evenings, and we have a lot of fun. We sometimes go to the movies, too!

Here's a photo of us at the movie theater – we're watching a horror movie! The second photo is of Ella and Sam. They're making a movie in the park – it's a comedy, so they're laughing. Sam is holding the camera in his hand. He makes great movies.

See you soon,

Viktor

1 Read Viktor's e-mail. In what order (1–4) does he do things a–d?

  a talk about the movie club   _____

  b close the e-mail   _____

  c describe some photos of the movie club _____

  d open the e-mail   _____

2 Viktor has some more photos of the movie club. Match the two parts of the sentences.

  1 In this photo, I'm with   _____   **a** and Sam with their cameras.

  2 Here's a photo of Ella   _____   **b** my friend, Bruce.

  3 Here's a photo of   _____   **c** sitting in the movie theater together.

  4 In this photo, we're   _____   **d** my favorite camera.

3 Complete the sentences with the personal pronouns in the box.

> I   you   he   she   it   we   they

  1 This is where the movie club meets. _____'s a small café near our college.

  2 Ella works part time. _____'s a waitress in a café.

  3 Ella and Sam sing and make music. _____'re really good actors, too.

  4 I'm with Sam. _____'re talking about ideas for our next movie.

  5 Sam has an older brother. _____'s in film school.

  6 What do you and your friends like doing? Do _____ enjoy watching movies?

  7 This is my camera. _____ love making movies with it!

4 Write an e-mail to a friend about a free-time activity you enjoy. Use the notes to help you plan your e-mail.

Paragraph 1: Ask your friend how he/she is.
Paragraph 2: Say what the activity is and why you like it.
Paragraph 3: Say when you do it and with who.
Paragraph 4: Describe two or three photos of your activity.

WRITING: Topic sentences

Where to buy clothes in Paris

A _____ But where can you go to get the best clothes? It's easy when you know the city. Here are some of my favorite places.

B _____ There are lots of them in many parts of the city and you can find really interesting things. You can buy costumes and jewelry from the 1960s and 1970s – they're cheap, too.

C _____ On the Champs Élysées, there are lots of small stores. You can buy beautiful shirts, pants, and jackets. Movie stars and pop stars shop there, too!

D _____ The Centre Beaugrenelle is my favorite! It's a wonderful place to meet friends and go for coffee, too. You can also go to the movies there.

E _____ There are many great cafés and parks in Paris – you can always find somewhere to relax after shopping! Montmartre is a great area for restaurants!

1 Read the text about clothes shopping in Paris. Match topic sentences 1–6 with paragraphs A–E. There is one extra sentence.

1 If you like old clothes, go to the markets. _____
2 There are also a lot of big shopping centers. _____
3 The best time to go shopping in Paris is in the spring. _____

4 Shopping can be hard work sometimes. _____
5 Everyone knows that Paris is a fantastic place for clothes shopping. _____
6 There are also some very expensive stores in Paris. _____

2 Choose the correct options to complete the sentences.

1 There are lots _____ good places to go shopping in my city.
   a on   **b** of   **c** at

2 The City Mall is a good place _____ fashionable clothes.
   a in   **b** of   **c** for

3 There are wonderful views of the city _____ the top floor of this shopping center.
   a to   **b** from   **c** in

4 If you _____ to find some really different clothes, go to the Saturday market.
   a want   **b** try   **c** take

5 Eating at the View Café is a great _____ to finish the day after shopping.
   a time   **b** way   **c** part

3 Write a description of some different places to go shopping in your town or city. Begin each paragraph with a topic sentence.

Paragraph 1: Describe the locations.
Paragraph 2: Say what you can buy there.
Paragraph 3: Say the best time to visit them.
Paragraph 4: Say what you like about the places.

WRITING: Planning and making notes

Last week, I went for a meal with my boyfriend. **¹***Before / Then* we went, I was really happy because I knew the restaurant was expensive and fashionable. I got dressed in my best clothes: a beautiful white dress and my best jewelry. **²***Then / First*, my boyfriend came to meet me at my house. It was a warm, sunny evening, and I felt fantastic.

Things didn't go well, though! The meal wasn't very good, and we had a terrible evening. **³***After / First*, the mushroom soup was cold. **⁴***Then / Before*, we had fish with rice and salad. The salad was terrible, too – I think it was a few days old.

⁵*Later / After* the meal, we had coffee. The waiter dropped a cup, and coffee went all over my white dress. I was so angry!

⁶*Later / First*, my boyfriend called me. He was really sorry! He sent flowers and chocolates to my house the next day. We are still together, but I don't want to go back to that restaurant – not ever!

1 Read Sandra's story. Choose the correct options for 1–6.

2 Number a–f in the order the things happened (1–6).

- **a** The waiter spilled coffee on Sandra. _____
- **b** Sandra ate some fish. _____
- **c** The soup wasn't good. _____
- **d** Sandra's boyfriend invited her to go for dinner. _____
- **e** Sandra's boyfriend sent presents to her. _____
- **f** Sandra's boyfriend called her. _____

3 Read the sentences. Complete the summary of Sandra's story.

1 The story happened _____ week.
2 At first, Sandra was happy because the _____ was expensive and fashionable.
3 At the start of the story, Sandra's boyfriend met her at her _____.
4 The meal wasn't good because the soup was _____ and the _____ was old.
5 After the meal, Sandra was angry because she had _____ on her dress.
6 Sandra and her boyfriend are still _____, but she doesn't want to go back to the restaurant again.

4 Think of a good or bad meal you ate. Write a story about it. Include the sequencers from exercise 1. Use the questions to make notes and plan your story.

1 When did it happen?
2 Where were you at the start?
3 What were the main events?
4 How did you feel at different times?
5 What happened in the end?

WRITING: Writing a description of a person

My favorite teacher is Mrs. Young. She's my music teacher. ¹_____ She has dark hair and happy eyes. She's always laughing! She's also a very good teacher, and she loves helping people. Mrs. Young lived with her aunt when she was a child. Her aunt was a musician and taught her to sing. Then, she learned to play the piano when she was three. ²_____ She was a student in college. At that time, she met her music band, The Dots. She played with them for many years. She stopped playing with her band. After that, she became a music teacher. She loved teaching young people, and she decided she wanted to teach music forever! She got a trumpet. After that, she started to play in a brass band. I admire Mrs. Young because she is a very good musician, and she works very hard. Her music classes are always fun. ³_____

By Mia

1 Read the description of Mrs. Young. Match the questions about her with notes a–e.

1	What does she teach?	_____	**a** always fun
2	What does she look like?	_____	**b** good musician, works hard
3	What did she learn to do when she was three years old?	_____	**c** to play the piano
4	Why does Mia admire her?	_____	**d** dark hair, happy eyes, always laughing
5	Why does Mia like her classes?	_____	**e** music

2 Complete 1–3 in the description with the sentences. There is one extra sentence.

a I love singing and playing the guitar because she always teaches us that the most important thing is to enjoy music.

b She's a really friendly person and everyone likes her.

c Music is a very popular school subject in the U.S.

d Later, she started to learn the guitar in elementary school.

3 Join the sentences about Mrs. Young using a clause with *when*. Write two versions for each sentence.

Example

Mrs Young lived with her aunt when she was a child./When she was a child, Mrs Young lived with her aunt.

1 She was a student in college. At that time, she met her music band, The Dots.

_____

2 She stopped playing with her band. After that, she became a music teacher.

_____

3 She got a trumpet. That's when she started to play in a brass band.

_____

4 Write about a teacher you admire. Think about the questions below. Include two sentences with *when*.

1 What does this teacher teach?

2 What does he/she look like?

3 What do you know about his/her life and achievements?

4 Why do you admire this teacher?

WRITING: Writing and replying to an invitation

I'm having a …

30th Birthday Trip!

I'd love you to join me!

We are going to go on a cruise in the Bahamas for three nights. We're going to stop in the capital, Nassau, and go sightseeing. The next day, we're going to go scuba diving on a small private island!

Where: Meet at the Miami cruise port on Dodge Island

When: June 18 – June 21

Please let me know if you can come!

Janine X

RSVP: janine95@pinkfish.com

Dear Janine,

Thanks so much for the invitation. What an exciting trip! I can definitely make it! I've never been to the Bahamas, but I would love to go there!

Can't wait to see you!

Lots of love,

Matt X

Dear Janine,

Thank you for the invitation. I'd love to come, but I don't have the money for the cruise. Also, I don't like traveling by boat because I get sick!

I hope you have a great time, and a very happy birthday.

Keep in touch.

Best wishes from Kylie

---

1 Read Janine's invitation and the two replies. Answer the questions.

1 Where is Janine going? _____

2 Who is going to go with her? _____

3 Who can't go? _____

2 Complete each phrase with one word.

1 I'm _____ a birthday trip!

2 Hope you _____ come!

3 Hope you can _____ it!

4 _____ reply.

5 I'm really _____, but we can't come.

3 Read Matt and Janine's online conversation. Choose the correct options to complete the sentences.

Matt	Hi Janine! I can't wait to go on the cruise.
Janine	I'm so happy you can come!
Matt	I'm going to bring some food for us to eat on the trip. Do you like ^{1}*a / – / the* chocolate?
Janine	I love it! Great idea. Thanks, Matt.
Matt	Is there ^{2}*a / – / the* bus in Miami to the cruise port?
Janine	No, there isn't. Let's take ^{3}*a / – / the* taxi. Where do you want to meet?
Matt	Let's meet at ^{4}*a / – / the* mall, then, at 2.30! Bye!

4 Reply to Janine's invitation. Use key phrases from exercises 1 and 2.

5 Imagine you are having a birthday trip party. Answer the questions below. Then write an invitation to Janine. Remember to use key phrases from exercises 1 and 2.

- Where are you going to go?
- When are you going to go?
- How are you going to get there?
- Where are you going to stay?

Richmond

58 St Aldates
Oxford
OX1 1ST
United Kingdom

Printed in Mexico
ISBN: 978-84-668-2639-6

© Richmond / Santillana Global S.L. 2017

Publishing Director: Deborah Tricker
Publisher: Luke Baxter
Editor: Helen Wendholt
Americanization: Deborah Goldblatt
Proofreaders: Fiona Hunt and Shannon Neill
Design Manager: Lorna Heaslip
Cover Design: Richmond
Design & Layout: Lorna Heaslip, Oliver Hutton, ColArt Design
Photo Researcher: Magdalena Mayo
Audio production: TEFL Audio

Illustrations:
Simon Clare

Photos:
J. Lucas; M. Sánchez; Prats i Camps; 123RF; ALAMY/
Blend Images, INTERFOTO, REUTERS, Keith Homan, MBI,
imageBROKER, Jose Luis Suerte, Harold Smith, Ian Allenden,
Peter Horree, MS Bretherton, Pulsar Images, andy lane,
Nano Calvo, Radharc Images, Westend61 GmbH, Colin
Underhill, Gianni Muratore, Mary Evans Picture Library,
Michael Wheatley, Alibi Productions, a-plus image bank,
ONOKY - Photononstop, Directphoto Collection, Arterra
Picture Library, Martin Thomas Photography, Agencja
Fotograficzna Caro, Cathy Topping, Blend Images - BUILT
Content, Geraint Lewis; GETTY IMAGES SALES SPAIN/
Thinkstock; I. PREYSLER; ISTOCKPHOTO/Getty Images Sales
Spain; SHUTTERSTOCK; SHUTTERSTOCK NETHERLANDS,B.V.;
SOUTHWEST NEWS/Leicester Mercury; ARCHIVO SANTILLANA

Cover Photo: istockphoto/wundervisuals

**We would like to thank the following reviewers for their
valuable feedback which has made Personal Best possible.
We extend our thanks to the many teachers and students not
mentioned here.**
Brad Bawtinheimer, Manuel Hidalgo, Paulo Dantas,
Diana Bermúdez, Laura Gutiérrez, Hardy Griffin, Angi Conti,
Christopher Morabito, Hande Kokce, Jorge Lobato, Leonardo
Mercato, Mercilinda Ortiz, Wendy López

The Publisher has made every effort to trace the owner of
copyright material; however, the Publisher will correct any
involuntary omission at the earliest opportunity.

Printed in Mexico by Impregráfica Digital, S.A. de C.V.
España 385, Col. San Nicolás Tolentino, C.P. 09850, Iztapalapa,
Ciudad de México.